▼ SCHOLASTIC GUIDES ▼

WRITING WITH STYLE

▼ SCHOLASTIC GUIDES ▼

WRITING WITH STYLE

• • • • • • • • • • • •

Sue Young

SCHOLASTIC
REFERENCE

Scholastic Inc.

NEW YORK SYDNEY

We wish to thank the student writers whose work, shown in this book, exemplifies writing with style: Lia Brezevar, Katherine Dunlap, Kwam Taylor Green, Amanda Kosanowich, Jason Knox, Ben Pred, Cassidy Ladden-Morwitz, Roopali Malhotra, Samantha Schlossman, and John Zagat. Thanks also to Barbara Mack for her guidance in the preparation of this manuscript.

Library of Congress Cataloging-in-Publication Data
Young, Sue,
       Writing with style / Sue Young.
           p. cm — (Scholastic guides)
       Includes index.
       Summary: Presents tips for writing interesting stories, passionate essays, and exciting reports, focusing on the elements of sentence structure, paragraph organization, grammar, usage, punctuation, and footnotes.

       1. Creative writing (Elementary education)—Juvenile literature. 2. English language—Composition and exercises—Study and teaching (Elementary)—Juvenile literature. [1. English language—Composition and exercises. 2. Creative Writing.] I. Title. II. Series.
LB1576.Y63 1997
372.6'23—dc20   96-8772
                                                 CIP
                                                 AC

ISBN 0-590-50977-2

12 11 10 9 8 7 6 5 4 3 2 1   7 8 9/9 0 1 2/0
                                                   12
Printed in the U.S.A.
First Scholastic printing, March 1997

TABLE OF CONTENTS

• • • • • • • • • • • • • • •

INTRODUCTION   9

CHAPTER I   PLANNING YOUR WORK

◆ Getting Started   11
   Find a place and time.   12
   Have your tools ready.   13
What are you writing?   14
Do your research.   16
   Brainstorm for ideas.   17
Before you begin, make a plan.   18
   Word Clusters   18
   Venn Diagrams   19
   Straightforward Outlines   20

CHAPTER II   PRODUCING YOUR WORK

◆ Beginning to Write   21
Writing well is a skill.   22
Build sentences and paragraphs.   22
   A sentence consists of a subject and a verb. 23
   A sentence always contains at least one thought. 23
   Start a new paragraph with each new idea.   23
   Building paragraphs takes careful work.   24
   Think of the sentence and the paragraph together. 26

Make a new paragraph each time the speaker changes. 28

In longer writing, use paragraphs as building blocks. 28

Clarity requires discipline. 30

Keep the action in one time frame. 30

As a rule, stick to the active voice. 31

Use the passive voice to emphasize the action
rather than the subject. 32

Use positive forms instead of negative ones. 33

Put up signposts: punctuation and headings. 34

Use headings or subtitles to guide the reader. 35

Beware of the run-on sentence. 37

Variety is the spice of life. 39

Use a thesaurus and a dictionary. 39

Every genre has a style. 40

Think about your audience. 40

Reports give information. 41

When a clear explanation is required,
make sure you know the answer first. 41

Footnotes credit sources. 44

Paraphrase; don't plagiarize. 46

Don't be boring. 46

Essays show you care. 46

Essays express your thoughts and opinions. 46

You may use the poet's tools. 54

Creating word images makes your writing
more vivid. 54

Rhymes are one of the poet's oldest tools. 56

Verses are the paragraphs of poetry. 59

Fiction is a figment of the imagination. 60
Your script can put words into people's mouths. 66
Scripts have a special format. 66
You need a cast. 67
Plays are organized by acts and scenes. 68
Take a break. 70

CHAPTER III   POLISHING YOUR WORK

◆ Fine-Tuning 71
Check the grammar of the sentence. 72
Subject and verb agree in number. 72
Number tells you how many people or things
you are writing about. 72
Pick the right pronoun for the job. 76
Punctuation holds it all together. 82
Sentences have to begin and end. 83
Commas separate certain words and phrases
from the rest of the sentence. 84
Apostrophes have a triple job. 89
Quotation marks identify spoken and borrowed words. 92
Standard spelling makes it readable. 94
Watch for confusing words and phrases. 95
Some verbs are tricky. 96
Prepositions make the right connections. 102
Adjectives and adverbs should be precise. 104
Substitute pronouns with care. 108

Editing makes it shine. 112
  This one's for your eyes only. 113
  Little things mean a lot. 113
  It's not in stone. 114
  Computers are wonderful—up to a point. 114
  The final draft is done. 116
  Hard work pays off. 118

CHAPTER IV   PRESENTING YOUR WORK

◆ Your Best Paper Forward 119
By hand or machine? 120
  Handwriting can be impressive. 120
  Typewriters still work. 121
  Word processors are nifty. 122
Presentation makes it neat. 123
  Format uniformly. 123
  Use spacing to organize your work. 124
  Organize by numbering. 125
  The table of contents goes up front. 126
Bibliographies back it up. 126
Make that final check. 129
  Reconsider your titles. 130
  Proofread. 130
  Add a top page. 131
  Need a folder? 131
Give yourself a pat on the back. 132

BIBLIOGRAPHY 133
INDEX 135

INTRODUCTION

· · · · · · · · · · · · · · · · ·

Writing With Style is about being the best writer you can be. Did you ever get a so-so grade on a paper that took you hours to write? What went wrong? Why didn't your work pay off?

Perhaps your time was not well spent. Good writing is *planned writing*. There are stages to go through — from preparation to presentation. Style is the result of the four **P**'s:

PLANNING where you will write, what form you will use, what research needs to be done in advance, which form of organization is best for your project.

PRODUCING a paper that reflects good grammar, clear thoughts, and appropriate genre style.

POLISHING your work by checking grammar, punctuation, spelling, and word choice.

PRESENTING your finest effort with uniform organization, proper source notations, and an attractive look that invites others to read on with pleasure.

Writing With Style makes it possible to get a head start on developing *your* style and becoming the writer you want to be.

Sue Young

Chapter I
PLANNING YOUR WORK

• • • • • • • • • • • • • • • • •

◆ **GETTING STARTED**

It's difficult to write well when you're staring at the clock instead of the page. Writing takes a lot of time. Plan ahead so that you have enough time to produce the best writing you can create.

If you play a sport, you know that you play best when your body is warmed up. Writing is a mental exercise in the same way that dance and football are physical exercises. Your mind needs to warm up in order for you to write well. The first few minutes of writing may be the most difficult. This is why it is important that you do not interrupt yourself while in the act of writing. If you do, you will have to warm up all over again.

> Writing well is a skill, much like
> other skills, in which preparation
> cannot be overlooked or faked.

Imagine for a moment that you are on the basketball court right in the middle of a layup, when you have to stop everything and look for something. When you've found it, can you go right back into the middle of the layup? Of course not. You have to wait for your chance to do another layup all over again. When you're in the middle of writing a report and you stop because a friend calls or you need to find an eraser, you are interrupting yourself from writing the best you can.

This chapter will focus on how to prepare to write by organizing yourself and your ideas before you start. You will be able to see that some of the writer's most important work is done before putting pen to paper.

✏ FIND A PLACE AND TIME.

Your workplace needs to be in an area that allows you to think. Separate yourself from the noise of radios and televisions and the voices of other people. A table or desk with good light puts you in the ideal position for thinking and writing. Clear the surface of clutter before sitting down to write. You wouldn't play basketball on a court strewn with half-full cans of soda, and you wouldn't pirouette across a floor cluttered with papers and pens. A clean and neat desk will help you to concentrate; a cluttered and messy desk will distract you.

Are you at your best right after you get home from school, or are you more alert early in the morning? Most people find that they concentrate best at a specific time of day. Give your-self every advantage by planning to write during that time.

✏ HAVE YOUR TOOLS READY.

If you're lucky enough to have your own writing desk or table, you will be able to organize it so that everything you need is at your fingertips.

If your workplace, however, is the kitchen table, you can keep most of your writing tools in a handy box or basket that can be set up at a moment's notice.

It's important to have your tools ready before you start to write because, if you don't, you will have to stop writing to go on a treasure hunt for your eraser or dictionary. This will waste time and will waste something even more precious: your train of thought.

Wherever you write, be sure that you have the following items close at hand:

- ◆ pens and pencils

- ◆ erasers

- ◆ writing paper and scratch paper

- ◆ reference books, such as a dictionary, thesaurus, encyclopedia, and, of course, *Writing With Style*

- ◆ a computer or a typewriter, if you use one

WHAT ARE YOU WRITING?

Now that you are stationed at your uncluttered desk with your mind clear and fresh and all your tools ready, it is time to get down to business.

Write your assignment at the top of the page or the computer screen. Make sure that you write it down accurately. Read the assignment over to yourself several times and decide exactly what it is that you are being asked to do.

Writing assignments take different forms. Below are the most common types of writing assignments and what they expect of the writer.

♦ **Reports** pass along information to others.

The report may be about something you have read or something you have seen or done. For example, you might report on *Little Women* by Louisa May Alcott or on your trip to City Hall.

♦ **Reviews** give your opinion about or reaction to an event or performance.

You might write a review of the movie *Indian in the Cupboard* or of a performance by the school orchestra. If you write a review (rather than a report) about a book you have read, most of the writing will concern your personal reaction.

◆ **Essays** are carefully shaped pieces of writing around a central theme or idea.

These may be factual statements or personal opinion. You might write an essay about the beginning of school or about the importance of recycling. Essays often attempt to persuade the reader of the writer's opinion, but they may simply paint a picture in words about an experience or feeling.

◆ **Stories** tell about real or imaginary happenings.

In nonfiction, you may describe a personal experience in the form of a story using details, remembered conversation, and your memory.

In fiction, you can explore the personalities of the characters and communicate the feel of the place, or setting, where the story is happening. The plot can be outlandish, exciting, and utterly untrue. For example, you might write a story called *My Trip to Mars.*

◆ **Plays** are stories told through dialogue and action.

What characters say and do move the action along.

◆ **Poems** are stories or thoughts written in strong rhythm with special attention to the sound of the words.

Think of poems as the most concentrated of writing forms. Poems are often written in rhyme, but other poems, sometimes called **free verse** or **blank verse,** have no rhymes.

DO YOUR RESEARCH.
• • • • • • • • • • • • • • • • •

Many writing assignments require research. Think about what you need to do for a particular assignment and organize your workload accordingly.

◆ For a **book report,** read the book and make notes of the main points and your reactions to them.

◆ For a **research report,** look up your topic in any and all reference sources you can find. Visit the local library and ask a librarian for assistance in finding the materials you need.

◆ For a **report on a science experiment,** use the notes you made while the experiment was in progress.

◆ For **creative writing,** such as short stories and poems, use your journal or other personal experiences for ideas that are yours alone. Talk to others about their experiences, which you can then interpret in your own words. When writing about relatives, you can arrange to interview them. Take notes during the interview and use them in your writing.

◆ For an **essay,** understand the assignment (to inform, to convince, to entertain). Depending on the purpose, do research, rely on your own experience, and decide how you feel about the topic.

✎ BRAINSTORM FOR IDEAS.

Now that you understand the assignment and have done your research, you can brainstorm for ideas about what you are going to write.

Brainstorming is a lot of fun. Write down whatever enters your head on the subject. Do not worry about spelling or grammar or incomplete sentences while brainstorming. No one will read this except you. The point is to get all your ideas onto paper, so that you can begin to work with them.

For instance, this list contains the highlights of a trip one student took to India.

- Left O'Hare International Airport early one June morning

- Traveled with my family

- Like 24 hours in a coma

- Landed at Indira Gandhi International in New Delhi at 3 A.M.

- Chaos of Indian cities contrasts with serene countryside

- Stop at Haradwar, holy city on the Ganges

- Why Hindus bathe in the Ganges

- I walk down marble steps through crowds of beggars and take the plunge

BEFORE YOU BEGIN, MAKE A PLAN.

• • • • • • • • • • • • • • • • •

Coaches always give a game plan to their players before sending them onto the field. Writers also need to organize what they're going to do before they try to do it. When you have brainstormed for ideas, look over your notes and organize your thoughts. Whether you use a formal outline or some other organizer, a plan is an essential step toward writing with style. You need one whether you're writing a book report, a poem, a letter to a grandparent, or your autobiography. Without an outline, you are likely to leave things out or jump from one idea to another too quickly. It may seem as though making a plan adds an extra step, but it will actually save you time. It is a lot easier to write what you have to say when you know what you have to say!

In an outline or graphic organizer, you decide what you are going to say without having to write down every word. Each paragraph then logically follows the next, and the writing itself becomes easier.

There are three popular ways of planning.

◆ **Word clusters** are good for poems and essays.

These word clusters form the organization of a poem Cassidy wrote:

Poems are like going through doors to rooms.

ROOM 1	ROOM 2	ROOM 3
golden sunlight	violets in every window	goldenrod
	always June	a silver snake
shadows	colored birds	water lilies
	spiderwebs	tiny people writing poetry

◆ **Venn diagrams** help you organize plots and facts and may help you see new relationships between various characters.

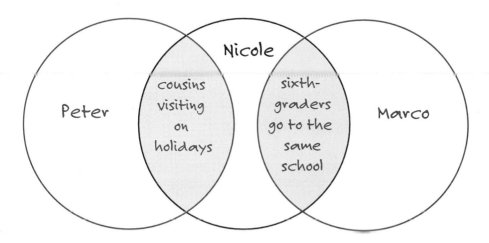

♦ **Straightforward outlines** help give form to reports and nonfiction stories. They may also help you build a structure for a play.

Here is an outline Ben wrote about the author Madeleine L'Engle.

I. Who is Madeleine L'Engle?
   A. What did she write?
   B. How did she become famous?
      1. A Wrinkle in Time
      2. An interesting point about the fate of her most famous book
II. Her childhood:
   A. She was considered stupid by her teachers and mocked by them.
   B. She was fiercely intelligent.
   C. No one, not even her mother, knew just how clever she was.
III. Madeleine today:
   1. Where does she live?
   2. What is she doing?

What you plan to write will help you decide which kind of plan works best. The important thing is to organize your ideas to ensure that you won't leave out any important information.

With your workplace organized, mind and spirit raring to go, and your plan perfected, you are ready for the fun part. Ready, set, write!

Chapter II
PRODUCING YOUR WORK

• • • • • • • • • • • • • • •

◆ BEGINNING TO WRITE

You have found the ideal place and time to work, completed your research, and made a plan. You can now begin to write. You know what you want to say and in what order you want to say it. But how will you put your ideas into words that will be exciting to read?

Writing well is a lot like learning how to play an instrument well. It requires practice. It doesn't matter how easily you write — the more you practice, the better you'll get. And just as a violin player learns from listening to the music of professional violinists, you can learn a lot about writing from reading the works of good authors.

> The more you read, the more you learn what you like and what you don't like. The more you write, the more your style develops.

You may often see things you wish you had written and begin to get an idea of how you want to write. But recognizing good writing does not mean that you imitate it. Reading should influence you but not tell you what words to use. That has to come from within you, yourself.

This chapter is designed to help you develop the skills and discipline you need to write well. No matter what form, or genre, your writing takes, there are time-tested ways of expressing your ideas clearly and convincingly with words that the reader will appreciate and remember.

WRITING WELL IS A SKILL.

A beginning pianist has to master the scales and learn to recognize the notes in order to play music. In the same way, a beginning writer must understand grammar and basic techniques of writing well in order to build interesting stories, essays, and exciting reports.

The following tips on basic usage will keep your writing strong, clear, and bold. They're easy to understand and easy to use!

BUILD SENTENCES AND PARAGRAPHS.

Sentences build on one another to create a paragraph that holds one idea or, in the case of story writing, one phase of action. To make your writing strong and polished, start with the basics: the sentence and the paragraph.

✏ **A SENTENCE CONSISTS OF A SUBJECT AND A VERB.**

Jessica (subject) is not a sentence, but

Jessica sang. (subject + verb) is a sentence.

✏ **A SENTENCE ALWAYS CONTAINS AT LEAST ONE THOUGHT.**

Jessica sang.

But a sentence can contain more than one thought:

At choir practice, Jessica sang and blinked back the tears as she thought of missing her favorite TV show.

(For more information about the grammar of the sentence, refer to Chapter III, Polishing Your Work.)

✏ **START A NEW PARAGRAPH WITH EACH NEW IDEA.**

In a story a new paragraph can mean a shift in action or time. In a report or an essay a new paragraph means that you are starting a new argument or idea. You show that you are beginning a new paragraph by indenting the first sentence of the new paragraph.

Suddenly and unexpectedly Jessica's father walked into the choir's practice room carrying a giant TV set!

You need another new paragraph when a different person is speaking.

"What on earth are you doing with that TV in here?" demanded Mrs. O'Connor.

And you need another one when the action switches back.

Without a word, Jessica's father plugged in the giant TV and tuned it to the channel so that Jessica could watch her beloved TV show.

✏ **BUILDING PARAGRAPHS TAKES CAREFUL WORK.**

In a report or essay, the sentences within the paragraph develop the idea in its topic sentence.

> Eating fast food is bad for you.
> It tastes good, but it is not healthful.
> Reports by consumer advocacy groups
> show that in many fast-food places
> basic standards of cleanliness are

not being practiced. The levels of salt and fat in fast foods are extremely high. I interviewed many fast-food workers who said they don't even eat the food they make because they know <u>how</u> it's made. For me that was enough reason to stop eating fast food in a hurry.

The topic sentence in the above paragraph is

Eating fast food is bad for you.

The middle of the paragraph gives reasons to support the writer's claim.

Reports by consumer advocacy groups show that in many fast-food places basic standards of cleanliness are not being practiced. The levels of salt and fat in fast foods are extremely high. I interviewed many fast-food workers who said they don't even eat the food they make because they know <u>how</u> it's made.

The final sentence concludes the ideas mentioned in the essay:

For me that was enough reason to
stop eating fast food in a hurry.

☞ **THINK OF THE SENTENCE AND THE
PARAGRAPH TOGETHER.**

A paragraph may consist of only a single sentence.

But none of the memories I have
described is my favorite.

This could be a complete paragraph. A single-sentence paragraph can be a dramatic way of catching your reader's attention. However, because you have a lot to say, most paragraphs, like the following ones, will have several sentences:

My favorite memory was the time
my granddad and I went fishing. The
weather was stormy but Poppa insisted
we go anyway. We drove to the lake
and boarded the rowboat. I was
scared because the winds were gale

force. Granddad remained stalwart. "This will make you strong," he told me, and only a half second later the wind blew him out of the boat, and he fell into the lake. I had to jump in to save him. It was hard to swim, but finally we made our way to the shore. "You're right," I said proudly. "This did make me strong."

Sometimes your work for an assignment will consist of a single paragraph. This is fine, but look over your writing and try to find a way to divide it into more than one paragraph. If it makes sense to do so, form several paragraphs. It's easier for the reader to read several small paragraphs than a single long paragraph.

My favorite memory was the time my granddad and I went fishing. The weather was stormy but Poppa insisted we go anyway. We drove to the lake and boarded the rowboat. I was scared because the winds were gale force. Granddad remained stalwart.

"This will make you strong," he told me, and only a half second later the wind blew him out of the boat, and he fell into the lake. I had to jump in to save him. It was hard to swim, but finally we made our way to the shore.

"You're right," I said proudly. "This did make me strong."

✏ **MAKE A NEW PARAGRAPH EACH TIME THE SPEAKER CHANGES.**

Indenting the speech of characters in your stories or report makes clear who is saying what.

"I hear that snow is expected tomorrow," I said brightly.

"Isn't that nice!" Dad replied.

"All the more reason to do your chores now so that tomorrow you can play," interjected Mother.

✏ **IN LONGER WRITING, USE PARAGRAPHS AS BUILDING BLOCKS.**

In the following story, John uses three paragraphs to help create a moving portrait of his grandmother.

It was always difficult to argue with Grandma, so I didn't bother and started picking currants as she had asked me to. Grandma told me that she used to pick currants with her father in Sea Cliff, Long Island, when she was a little girl. She also told me about picking blueberries on the islands of Elk Lake in the Adirondacks. I told Grandma that I had picked raspberries along the trails at Elk Lake that summer and those raspberries tasted better than any others I had ever eaten. She smiled.

We continued to pick currants until the last bucket was completely full. I asked Grandma why she was going to make so much jelly. She said that she liked to give her own jelly to her friends whenever she went to visit. I helped her carry the buckets up to her house, but I never saw her make the jelly. I fell asleep before she started.

The next morning there were rows of small jars of all kinds and sizes

filled with fresh jelly on the table
next to the stove. The biggest jar
was labeled "For John. My best picker.
Love, Grandma." It was delicious.

In paragraph one, John sets the scene for his memory: His grandmother has asked him to pick currants with her and, even though he doesn't want to, he does. While picking together, he and his grandmother swap stories about berry picking.

In paragraph two, the picking is finished and John falls asleep before he can help his grandma turn the currants into jelly.

In paragraph three, John wakes to find the currants transformed into jelly as if by magic and a lovely present from his grandmother, thanking him for their time together.

CLARITY REQUIRES DISCIPLINE.

✏ **KEEP THE ACTION IN ONE TIME FRAME.**

When you are **telling** a story in conversation, you might find that you often change tenses for a slangy effect.

I went to my mom, "Like I need to
eat some potato chips." And she goes,
"Absolutely not!"

or

> I go to the dance and I'm standing
> there all alone when this friend of
> my brother's came up to me and asks
> me to dance!

This is very lazy English when it is spoken. When it is written down and read, this switching of verb tenses is positively dizzying!

In this case, **asked** and **replied** are in the past tense:

> I asked my mom, "May I have some
> potato chips?" And she <u>replied</u>
> "Absolutely not!"

and

> I went to the dance. I was all alone
> when a friend of my brother's came
> up to me and <u>asked</u> me to dance.

✏ AS A RULE, STICK TO THE ACTIVE VOICE.

The active, direct account is clearer than the passive, or "as told to," voice and much more lively. Which sentence makes you want to read more?

At the beginning of the novel, we are introduced to Gene as a shy and dependent person.

or

Gene is shy and dependent at the beginning of the novel.

By making the subject of the sentence the source of the action instead of the recipient of the action, you make the sentence itself bolder, more dramatic, and more interesting.

☞ **USE THE PASSIVE VOICE TO EMPHASIZE THE ACTION RATHER THAN THE SUBJECT.**

The sentence

Abraham Lincoln was assassinated.
(subject)   (passive verb)

emphasizes the fact that President Lincoln was assassinated.
    Writing the same sentence with an active verb gives a different emphasis.

John Wilkes Booth   assassinated   Lincoln.
(subject)   (verb)   (object)

In the active sentence, the murderer is emphasized more than Lincoln himself.

➱ **USE POSITIVE FORMS INSTEAD OF NEGATIVE ONES.**

Clear writing is writing that says exactly what it means. For this reason, a positive statement —

Jasper **was ecstatic** when he joined Little League.

is stronger than the negative form:

Jasper **was not unhappy** when he joined Little League.

The negative form can be used to create a sarcastic or understated tone.

Harry **was not disappointed** when the teacher called on somconc clsc.

Using the negative here suggests that you are stating the obvious in a sly, clever way. You should use it only occasionally for effect.

PUT UP SIGNPOSTS: PUNCTUATION AND HEADINGS.

Punctuation and headings help guide readers through your words. Punctuation can make the difference in meaning between

We're going to the football game.

and

We're going to the football game?

and

We're going to the football game!

Punctuation can also help clarify a sentence that could otherwise be misunderstood. Notice the crucial role a comma plays in the following sentence.

Paul passed the popcorn to Alisa, and Jack, who had been waiting in the lobby, came in to the theater and sat down.

Now read the same sentence without the comma and notice the confusion caused by its absence.

Paul passed the popcorn to Alisa and Jack, who had been waiting in the lobby, came in to the theater and sat down.

Without the comma after *"Alisa,"* we would have thought that Paul has passed the popcorn to Alisa *and* Jack and then as we continued to read the rest of the sentence, we would have been thoroughly confused.

For a complete review of punctuation, go to Chapter III, Polishing Your Work.

✏ ## USE HEADINGS OR SUBTITLES TO GUIDE THE READER.

Headings or subtitles keep the reader focused on what you have to say. They may also keep *you* focused on what you need to say. You can come up with titles for each paragraph you write by taking them from your outline. When you have finished writing, you may take the titles out or leave them in, depending on how much they add to the overall presentation.

Do you remember Ben's outline from Chapter I (page 20)? This is how his report looked.

Madeleine L'Engle
Author — Doreen Gonzales

Madeleine L'Engle is a children's writer, a very good children's author. She loves her family (and still does). One day she decided to write a book called A Wrinkle in Time. Publishers turned it down. She finally told her agent that "the story is too peculiar. No one will ever publish it. . . ."[1] Then, "one morning . . . Ruth Gagliardo told Madeleine that A Wrinkle in Time had won the 1963 Newbery Medal."[2] Madeleine had written for a long time. After nearly three decades of writing, . . . her . . . novel had won the Newbery Medal and she was very happy. (Wouldn't you be?)

Her Childhood

Madeleine was considered stupid as a child. Once, her poem won first prize in her school contest, and her teacher didn't believe she had written it. "Madeleine isn't bright . . . She must have copied it."[3] Her teacher also said she was "clumsy and dumb."[4] The teacher also held up Madeleine's papers and laughed at them in front of the class. Now Madeleine's "stupid" work is considered to be fine writing.

Madeleine was also very observant. Nobody guessed how

keenly Madeleine observed things
during family trips, not even her
mother. Years later, Madeleine
described them in detail.

Madeleine Today

Today, Madeleine lives in New York.
She has three children and three
grandchildren. She was married to
Hugh Franklin, who was an actor. He
died in 1986 of cancer. Madeleine
(surprise, surprise!) wrote a book about
their life together. Madeleine has
written almost thirty books to date,
and I hope she will continue.

✏ BEWARE OF THE RUN-ON SENTENCE.

Run-on sentences are two sentences joined together without punctuation or with just a comma. Here is one:

Odysseus left the Lotus Eaters, he visited the Cyclops and
took a group of men into one of the many caves where they
met a Cyclops who ate two men and went to sleep.

One simple way to correct this sentence is to substitute a period for the comma.

Odysseus left the Lotus Eaters. He visited the Cyclops and took a group of men into one of the many caves where they met a Cyclops who ate two men and went to sleep.

But you could turn the first part into a dependent clause.

After Odysseus left the Lotus Eaters, he visited the Cyclops and took a group of men into one of the many caves where they met a Cyclops who ate two men and went to sleep.

You might also break the passage into shorter sentences.

After Odysseus left the Lotus Eaters, he visited the Cyclops. He took a group of men into one of the many caves. There they met a Cyclops who ate two men and went to sleep.

Only you know which style works for you. The important thing is that every sentence has a complete thought with a subject and a verb.

Style suggestion:
Always try to get at the essence of what you have to say. It may take time to rewrite sentences, but they will be clearer and more readable when you do.

✏ **VARIETY IS THE SPICE OF LIFE.**

In general, good writers use active verbs, short sentences, and positive statements. But there are exceptions to all these rules. You will sometimes want to use the passive voice or the negative form, and write long, winding sentences. Every style rule is made to be broken *occasionally* to keep the reader from getting bored. Take care not to break rules of grammar while you are at it! (For help with grammar, go to Chapter III: Polishing Your Work.)

USE A THESAURUS AND A DICTIONARY.

Writing gives you the chance to think in a formal way. You might find that you do not always have the right words to say what you mean. Use a thesaurus to enlarge your vocabulary. English is a colorful language with thousands of choices for describing things. For instance, a stream of water can be described as trickling, seeping, bubbling, babbling, racing, cascading, scampering, silent, rushing, gushing, or dancing, to name a few. Only *you* know which word best portrays the stream you have in mind. Maybe you'll find a word that you haven't thought about.

A dictionary is better than a thesaurus for making sure you are using a particular word correctly and that it is spelled right.

EVERY GENRE HAS A STYLE.
●●●●●●●●●●●●●●●●

Your writing style will vary with the kind of writing you do. Writing a report is very different from writing a story, so different rules of style apply. For example, you might write a story or play in which a character says,

"This is not very cool. I'm like really bored."

That may be considered good fictional writing, because it sounds like something that someone might actually say. But the same kind of style does not work when you write up your science experiment. The sentence

The liquid turned this really cool color.

would be poor writing. In writing about science, precision and observation are praised, not the way you use slang. The reader (perhaps your teacher) wants to know exactly what color the liquid turned — bright pink or pale blue.

✏ **THINK ABOUT YOUR AUDIENCE.**

Another key question in choosing a style for an assignment is "Who will read this?" If you are writing a report that you will read to the entire class, you will want to write in such a way as to keep your classmates and your teacher interested. But if you are writing a report that only your teacher will read, your tone — and the content — may change. A movie review for the

40 ....

school newspaper will not have the same tone as a letter to your grandparents. Different readers want to know different things.

You might also think about the effect you want your writing to have on the reader. Do you want to entertain or inform? Do you want to move your audience to tears or spasms of laughter? Do you want to create an atmosphere of suspense? Or should the reader immediately volunteer to work on the cause you feel so passionately about? Whatever you intend, keep it in mind as you write.

REPORTS GIVE INFORMATION.

☞ **WHEN A CLEAR EXPLANATION IS REQUIRED, MAKE SURE YOU KNOW THE ANSWER FIRST.**

A very common assignment is to explain something to the reader. You may be asked to show that you understand what you have read in a book or what you have done in a science experiment. Or you may be asked to research a topic in several sources and write a single report. Making an outline will help you decide what you really understand and what still seems unclear. You will have to find the answers for yourself before you can put them into writing. If you are vague, your writing will sound dull and confusing. No matter what fancy words you choose, they will never cover up a lack of understanding. Make the effort to get real answers. If your notes are unclear, return to the source until you understand exactly.

Good explanations are easily understood.

When you're satisfied that you have all the information you need, strive to be crystal clear in your writing. You'll show your teacher how much attention you paid, and your writing will make sense.

Again, a big key to writing well is taking the *time* to do so. It may be easier to write

> Sandy and I stood over the test tube. The test tube was on this thing called a Bunsen burner. Then I poured the purple stuff in. It smelled bad. That's when we noticed the vinegar had turned this sort of red color. Cool.

But it's much better to read

> Today's experiment was to discover what would happen when you add citric acid to vinegar while the vinegar was being heated.
>
> 1. Sandy and I carefully placed our plastic goggles over our eyes and put on plastic gloves as a safety measure in the event of an accident with the chemicals.

2. Sandy filled the test tube with four ounces of household vinegar.

3. I slowly turned the gas switch on the Bunsen burner, struck a match, and lit the burner.

4. Sandy used the tongs to place the test tube over the flame. The liquid began to bubble, which meant it had reached boiling temperature.

5. I measured an ounce of citric acid, which was purple, and poured it into the vinegar.

6. For a split second the mixture caught fire because of the reaction between the two chemicals. Then the flame went out, and what remained was a cherry-pink liquid — the brightest color I think I have ever seen.

   In the first passage, which is carelessly written, the reader does not know what Sandy and the writer are doing and certainly won't know why. In the second passage, the writer gives us the details. We know the purpose of the experiment and how it was conducted — step-by-step. With this report, we could repeat the experiment exactly as the students did it. Detail and clarity work together to make the writing strong.

Sources give you information, but the writing is up to you.

When you get information from a book or the Internet or by interviewing someone, you may take notes using the words of the source. Before you begin to write, you should read over the notes to make sure you understand them. Next, you demonstrate that you understand the information by putting the facts and ideas into your own words. (This is sometimes called **paraphrasing.**)

✏ **FOOTNOTES CREDIT SOURCES.**

If you use someone else's words, put them in quotation marks and tell the reader who said them. In his report on the biography of Madeleine L'Engle, Ben used only one book but he placed quotation marks around the parts he copied directly and used little numbers to mark each one. Then, at the end, he listed the source. These are called **footnotes,** and you may use them to quote one, or several, sources.

Ben's footnotes for the report on Madeleine L'Engle's biography (see page 35) looked like this.

1. Doreen Gonzales, <u>Madeleine L'Engle</u>, New York, Macmillan Publishing Co. 1991, p. 79.

2. Gonzales, p. 80.
3. Gonzales, p. 25.
4. Gonzales, p. 22.

If Ben had used more than one source, each one would have been listed just like his first footnote. In more academic reports, writers often use the Latin term *op. cit.,* for a later reference to the same book, as in

2. Gonzales, op. cit., p. 80.

And if they quote the same book in the very next reference, they use

3. Ibid. p. 4.

Footnotes are only one way for crediting an author. For example, Ben might have written

One day she decided to write a book called <u>A Wrinkle in Time</u>. Publishers turned it down. She finally told her agent that "the story is too peculiar. No one will ever publish it . . ." (Gonzalez, p. 79)

✏ ## PARAPHRASE; DON'T PLAGIARIZE.

The ideas and information of other people paraphrased and mixed with other sources throughout a report do not need direct quotations, but you should list all your sources in a separate bibliography. (See Chapter IV, Presenting Your Work, page 126.)

Plagiarism means copying the ideas and words of others. Don't do it! It's worse than writing badly. It's cheating.

✏ ## DON'T BE BORING.

You should make your readers feel that what you are reporting is interesting and important. The only way the reader will feel this is if you yourself find the subject interesting and important. If you are bored by a topic, look more closely to find at least one part that you find interesting. Emphasize what is interesting to you, and you will be sure to write convincingly about it. Furthermore, your report will be original.

ESSAYS SHOW YOU CARE.

✏ ## ESSAYS EXPRESS YOUR THOUGHTS AND OPINIONS.

In a report, you work to explain information clearly and without an opinion. In an essay, you try to persuade the reader that your ideas are correct and meaningful. Whether your essay is about *Little Women*, nuclear waste, or pop music, you'll want your ideas to be clear and your writing to be engaging. A good tip to keep in mind is:

If your ideas don't make sense to you, they won't make sense to anyone else.

An outline or word clusters are useful when organizing an essay. (See Chapter I, Planning Your Work, page 18.) A strong essay should include about three good arguments or ideas. It's better to develop a few ideas fully than to throw lots of half-baked notions at the reader. You won't make your essay better by having a long list of ideas.

Opening paragraphs should be strong.

In the opening paragraph of an essay, you want to grab the reader by the shirt collar and make her or him pay attention to what you've got to say. You do this by finding a first sentence that is direct, strong, and to the point. Ben had this to say about a novel he read.

> In my opinion, the biggest conflict in Lord of the Flies was person versus person. The conflict of Ralph and Jack (good versus evil) dominated the story. It was one of the reasons Jack's tribe was against Ralph. The other reason was that Jack always wanted

to be the best. In this essay
I will further explain the central
conflicts of <u>Lord of the Flies</u>.

In the first paragraph you want to state the thrust of your essay and let the reader know what your opinions are. For the rest of the essay you will share with the reader good reasons why he or she should agree with you.

By the end of the first paragraph the reader should understand what you are writing about and should be interested enough to want to read more. The smooth and flowing style of your writing will make reading your essay a pleasure.

After you state your opinion, back it up.

In another book report, Ben does a good job of explaining his opinion.

What was unique about the gorilla part in <u>Congo</u> was that in most science fiction novels, the author creates this whole, totally different reality. Everything in it is different. However, in <u>Congo</u>, a lot — actually everything — is the same except that he took a species of animal and gave it superior intelligence. He didn't make many major changes except that.

> I enjoyed the book a lot because
> it is believable and original. This is
> not true of most science fiction
> books I've read.

In a few sentences, we've learned that Ben liked this book and know why he did. In a good essay, the writer focuses his ideas around his thoughts and opinions, rather than the facts. That doesn't mean the facts don't count. You must understand and explain the facts if you want your opinion to sound informed.

Play devil's advocate: Try to disagree with yourself.
A devil's advocate is someone who preaches the opposite of what is believed to be right. Suppose your essay contains three ideas you're proud to say that you've thought up all by yourself. Test their mettle. Read over your essay and try to disagree with yourself.
If you wrote

> Little Women is a good book.
> The character of Jo is the most
> interesting.

ask yourself why Jo is the most interesting character to you. This may lead to your writing

> Little Women is a good book
> with very interesting characters,

but it was Jo that most caught my imagination because she is a tomboy and wants to be a writer.

Or if you were writing

An advertisement for the nuclear energy industry claims that nuclear energy is the cleanest form of energy, but I disagree. It's amazing how people just ignore the dangers of nuclear waste.

you could ask yourself why, if it's such a big problem, do people ignore it? While asking that question you might realize that not everyone ignores the problem of nuclear waste. You don't! And why is that? Then you might come up with something like this:

Nuclear waste is a big problem, but most people just ignore it. Maybe this is because they don't know much about it. I became interested in nuclear waste during my Environmental Science class. I learned that the waste created by burning nuclear fuel will be dangerous, even deadly, for many, many generations. That is why some people are concerned about whether there is any really safe place to dispose of nuclear waste. Perhaps if more people knew the dangers, they would demand that their power companies use other forms of energy or put more research into finding a way to burn nuclear fuels more efficiently with less waste.

Playing devil's advocate with your own writing enriches your ideas. You may even change your mind about something and come up with better, stronger opinions. At the very least, you will make your writing more interesting. It may take extra time — but it's worth it. The proof will be in your writing!

Beware of generalizations.

A **generalization** is a sweeping statement that is almost certainly not true — even though people tend to make generalizations with a very confident tone.

Some generalizations you may have heard, or even said, are:

90210 will always be my favorite show — even when I'm 80 years old.

Mexican food is always spicy and hot.

The Smiths, who live next door, are all alike.

Boys are obnoxious.

All girls love the color pink.

I hate vegetables.

I'll never wear fuchsia.

It feels very dramatic to say such exaggerated things — but they sound pretty silly (and can make you appear uninformed). Of course, *90210* will not be your favorite show throughout your life! And you can't really hate every single vegetable that ever sat on your plate — or those vegetables you have yet to try.

Say precisely what you think. It may sound less dramatic than a sweeping statement, but it will definitely carry more power.

Generalization:

90210 will always be my favorite show.

Precision:

Right now, *90210* is my favorite show.

Closing paragraphs pull it together.

In the closing paragraph of an essay, bring together all your ideas. The closing paragraph should complement the opening paragraph. You should be able to say in the final paragraph that you fulfilled the promises you made in your opening paragraph.

In the conclusion of this essay about *Tom Sawyer*, Lia sums up her ideas about the main character.

> Tom does break rules and makes a lot of trouble, but there is more good to him than a lot of people think. He shows sympathy and kindness in most of his actions. It may take a lot of work to get the few words, "I love you," out of his mouth, but it is possible. When Tom lies to Aunt Polly about the dream he had, Aunt Polly cries over how much he doesn't care enough to show her respect. Tom replies, "Now auntie, you know I do care for you." He is always a good friend to Huck Finn, while nobody else pays attention to him. Tom may be mischievous, but at heart he is a good boy.

YOU MAY USE THE POET'S TOOLS.
• • • • • • • • • • • • • • • • •

✏ ### CREATING WORD IMAGES MAKES YOUR WRITING MORE VIVID.

When you write poetry, you want to be careful and precise with every word. There are several ways you can use words to make them create a mental picture for the writer. We call these word pictures **imagery.** While poets use imagery most often, it can also bring grace to your prose.

Use similes and metaphors to compare objects and ideas.

In a **simile,** you can compare something you are writing about with something else the reader will recognize.

Kwam writes

> A plane dropped bombs <u>like</u> watermelons from the sky.

Lia writes

> That useless life did nothing, just sat around <u>like</u> a hanger with no coat.

Metaphors are much like similes, but they do not use **like** or **as.**

Lia writes

> Silence is the winter
>
> It is the snow
>
> Silence is the whiteness

Crash! Bang! It's onomatopoeia.
Onomatopoeia uses words to imitate real sounds.
Lia writes

> Milk, so ordinary, so plain
>
> But what would life be
> without milk
>
> Mooooooooo! Yep, that's where
> it all starts

And Ben writes

> Wham! I hear as the ball hits
> the floor.
>
> Parents talking; kids yelling.
>
> The silent swish of the basket.
> Clank.

Alliteration

The repetition of the same sound at the beginning of two or more words next to or near each other is called **alliteration.**

Lia writes

> Come with me to the wet, windy,
> wond'rous land.

Personification makes things "human."

Personification means giving human qualities to things that are not human.

Here, Ellen writes in the voice of a piece of bread being used in a sandwich.

> The slice lay moaning as the finger
> crushed its center.

And Cassidy writes

> The water lily weeps
> and makes a pool for the tiniest bugs.

✏ RHYMES ARE ONE OF THE POET'S OLDEST TOOLS.

Probably the first poems you heard were written in rhyme. Rhymes are formed by the vowel sounds at the end of words.

A perfect rhyme is formed when words have the same end sound preceded by a different consonant.

Kwam writes

> I think you're so humble
> And you never mumble

And Lia writes

> Down, down, down the stairs
> Went the table and the chairs

These are perfect rhymes, but many people make rhymes with less than perfect sounds. For example, they might rhyme the words *charm* and *false alarm*. These are called slant rhymes and they are often used in songs and rap. For new ideas on words that rhyme, you might consult *The Scholastic Rhyming Dictionary.*

Rhyming patterns

Poets write rhymes in many patterns. Some of the simplest are the **couplet,** in which two lines rhyme, one after the other.

Jason writes

> Willie Worm's home was an apple tree.
> His family was content as worms can be.

In this rhyme scheme, every other line rhymes. It's called a,b,a,b.

Samantha writes

> We're HOME ALONE, Hurray! Hurray! (a)
>
> With no one to tell us, "Stop!" (b)
>
> With junk food and some games to play (a)
>
> We'll party 'til we drop. (b)

There are many other rhyme patterns, some of which can be very complicated. But you can have fun with rhymes without using a formal pattern, as Kwam does here.

> When I grow up
>
> I want to be an astronaut.
>
> I want to fly
>
> high
>
> up in the sky,
>
> into space.
>
> First I'd go to Jupiter,
>
> Then I'd go to Pluto.
>
> Then I'd come back
>
> To relax.

✏ **VERSES ARE THE PARAGRAPHS OF POETRY.**

Poems are written in **verses,** rather than paragraphs. But as with prose, the writer shapes each verse around a single idea. Katherine writes

> I am sheltered.
>
> When I walk out of my house,
>
> I am not stepping into a society of violence.
>
> I am not like others who live in an environment
>
> where kids carry guns just for protection
>
> to walk to school.

In another verse, she writes

> I am sheltered.
>
> I do not wake up in the morning wondering if I will have food to eat.
>
> Without a thought, I go downstairs to grab a snack
>
> while some children are starving.

At the conclusion of her poem, she sums up her thoughts:

I take so many things for granted.
I cannot even comprehend

what life is like for some of
these people.

We are all living in the same world,
yet we all view it differently.

I hear about the ugliness of the
world, but I do not see it.

I hear about hate, violence,
starvation, war, poverty,

but it is not happening to me.

I am secure in my surroundings

where I am kept innocent and
ignorant,

Ignorant of what the world is like

for the ones who are suffering.

I am sheltered.

FICTION IS A FIGMENT OF THE IMAGINATION.
• • • • • • • • • • • • • • • • •

When you write fiction, the story is yours to shape. The
people in your fiction, the characters, may be entirely made-up,

or they may be based on real people. The place, or setting, in which the story takes place may be down the street — or in another galaxy. It's up to you. The idea is to create a believable situation in which your story can take place. Since you create the characters and the setting, it's up to you to make sure that they make sense to the reader. If your story takes place on a desert island, the main character will not be able to call out for pizza. You create a situation or problem that is the crux of your story. Then you tell the story in such a way that builds to a climax and that has your readers eager to hear what is going to happen. Finally, you bring all the pieces together in the end, which is often called the **resolution.** The story can be one page long or many chapters. It's all up to you.

In this short story, the leading character, or **protagonist,** is a girl. Cassidy begins

> My best friend Alice was moving away. Okay, so I was feeling a little glum. But hey, isn't everybody? I mean it's not every day that your lifelong companion is moving away forever. You can't exactly celebrate the moment, can you?
>
> Let me begin at the beginning.

Next, Cassidy tells us a bit about the protagonist.

> I know, I know. Whiney opening, huh? My name is Amanda Wikstaff. I'm twelve years old. I have short, blond hair, a slender figure, and chocolate brown eyes. My nose is very short. Too short. I keep pulling at it but nothing ever happens.

Now that we know a little bit about Amanda, we meet her family.

> Mom says I'm a little small for my age. In other words, I'm a shrimp. But I don't care. My ten-year-old brother Doug always calls me Tubs. I don't know why. I'm very skinny for my age. But I guess it's just his way of showing he doesn't know anything.

And skillfully, Cassidy moves back to the character's problem.

> Anyway, my best friend is moving away and there is nothing I can do about it. My mom said, "You'll always find new friends."

I screamed at her, "That's what you think!" Then I ran up to my room and slammed the door.

Before long, Amanda has jumped on her bike and pedaled over to Alice's house for one last good-bye. Instead, she finds a FOR RENT sign on the door. Here's what happens next.

With a defeated sigh, I sank to the ground. I let out a low moan. Not only would I never see her again, but I didn't even get to say good-bye either!

Suddenly, someone tapped me on the shoulder. I stared into the face of a hideous monster. Green globs dripped from its snoutlike nose. Blood-spattered fangs opened and shut. Ants were strewn in the green monster's hair. I stared wide-eyed into the creature's blue eyes, and suddenly, I recognized them.

"Doug!" I roared, "you jerk!"

As it turns out, Doug is wearing a mask. Furious, Amanda then pedals back home and phones another girl, Katy. She invites her for a sleepover.

Later that night, snickering softly to ourselves, Katy and I made our way back to my room and opened my closet door. I lay on the floor with my head and arms half hidden inside the closet and only my legs and slippers showing. Then I closed my eyes and waited while Katy woke Doug. A few seconds later, Doug entered my room. When he saw me sprawled out on the floor, he gave a shriek of terror and ran to my parents' room. We chuckled to ourselves. It had worked. He had run from terror. Pure terror. Now Doug and I were even.

Amanda's parents wake up and tell everybody to settle down, and they go to sleep. Here's how Cassidy ends her story.

The next morning, I swigged a glass of orange juice and gulped down my cornflakes. Then I ran a brush through my short blond hair. I grabbed my windbreaker and ran outside. Then I slipped on my Rollerblades and skated with

Katy to her house. The sun felt good on my face. Katy and I were good friends now that Alice was gone. Before, all three of us, Katy, Alice, and I, had been known as the gruesome threesome. And now we would be known as the gruesome twosome.

Although the fiction writer is creating a story, many of the stylistic devices that make any writing smooth are put to good use. Cassidy tells her story in short, crisp sentences. She uses the active voice (see page 32) and allows the characters to speak in carefully punctuated dialogue. Her sentences build to paragraphs that have a beginning, a middle, and an end — just as her story does.

You may notice that Amanda usually speaks in a certain tone. Whenever we read it, we know she is speaking.

I know, I know. Whiney opening. . . . Anyway, my best friend is moving away and there is nothing I can do about it. Not only would I never see her again, but I didn't even get to say good-bye either!

YOUR SCRIPT CAN PUT WORDS INTO PEOPLE'S MOUTHS.

Most writers assume that the words they write will be read or listened to exactly as they express them. But writers who want their work produced onstage or in movies or on television write in a different style. A script contains words that will be spoken. Other parts of the writer's work are invisible to the audience — but necessary to the story.

✐ SCRIPTS HAVE A SPECIAL FORMAT.

Scripts for plays or films follow a different form from other writing. Part of a script is **dialogue,** which the characters will speak. But a scriptwriter must also be concerned with giving other people — producers, directors, actors, makeup experts and wardrobe people, light and (sometimes) camera crews — instructions for the overall effect the play should create.

Some of the other parts of the script include:

- ◆ **the cast:** a list of all the characters with descriptions of those people
- ◆ **the setting:** a detailed description of where each part of the script takes place
- ◆ **stage instructions:** where the actors should be when they speak to each other on stage, how they should speak, what they should do

- **the prologue:** what the writer wants the audience to know about what it is going to hear and see.

- **the epilogue:** action that takes place after the story shown in the play or film is completed, or the writer's thoughts about the meaning of the play.

☞ YOU NEED A CAST.

A script begins with a list of all the characters who will appear. In this script for television, Amanda lists her characters with a brief description of each.

Mike's Grandfather: He owned the house that Mike's parents have kept up these past years. He disappeared about seven years ago, and by now all have given up hope of ever finding him.

Mike: He is a teenager with a passion for adventure. He is very athletic. He does not take great responsibility well, though.

Joe: He is another teenager who is very intelligent and knows how to take charge in stressful situations.

Ashley: She is fifteen, the same age as Mike and Joe. She is very quiet and smart and able to assess strange situations.

Breanne: She is a very talkative girl and is very obsessed with her looks.

The Phantom: He is a faceless man who is the definition of evil. To him it matters little whom he hurts as long as he gets what he wants.

If you were a director or an actor looking for a part, reading the list of characters would be a big help to you. If you see a stage play, you will probably find this list in your program, but if you watch this play on television or in a movie, chances are you won't see this list until the credits roll at the end.

✏ **PLAYS ARE ORGANIZED BY ACTS AND SCENES.**

In a brief script, all the action can frequently be contained within one act. But in a longer script, the action may be broken into acts and scenes, just as books are broken into chapters and paragraphs. New acts and new scenes give the crew time to change scenery and actors the opportunity to change costumes.

In Scene 1 of her play's first act, Amanda gives only brief staging directions.

Act 1: Scene 1

[The time is seven years ago. Today Mike's grandfather enters the attic. Outside, lightning flashes. Mike's grandfather makes his way through the dusty clutter until he comes to a splendid, Victorian, full-length mirror. The mirror appears to be glowing. Lightning flashes again, and Mike's grandfather is gone.]

Notice that Amanda put these directions inside brackets. That signals to the reader that the words are not being spoken.

Settings tell where the writer envisions the action taking place.

In Scene 2 of Amanda's script, the action moves to another setting. Again, she gives the reader the information in brackets.

> [We see a street in a current-day Massachusetts town. The houses along the street are old, Victorian ones. You look farther down the street and see four kids riding their bikes. The sky is dark, and thunder can be heard in the distance.]

Notice how Amanda uses the setting to succinctly describe modern times while using the architecture (read Gothic) and the weather to signal that something bad could be happening any minute.

Dialogue moves the action along.

As the characters begin to speak, the action starts rolling.

> Mike [shouts]: Ashley, Breanne, would you two hurry up! I'd like to get to my grandpa's before this storm sets in!

Joe: Those two are so slow. [The girls catch up with them.]

Ashley [offended]: Are not. We're better than you guys are at a lot of things.

Breanne: Hey, like, where are we going, again?

Joe [sounding quite annoyed]: For the millionth time, we are going to Mike's grandpa's house. Got it?

Each act tells a part of the story.

Amanda's play continues for three acts. Many things happen before Mike's grandfather is rescued from the mirror where he is trapped. The script closes with shattered glass on the floor — and the image of the phantom still reflected.

TAKE A BREAK.

Whew! You finally put your ideas onto paper. No matter what you produced — a report, an essay, a story, a poem, or a play — it's time to step away. Go for a walk, play with the dog, or call a friend. If you've given yourself enough time, you may want to wait until tomorrow to look at your work again. If you have less time, do something else — your math homework, for example — to clear your head before you begin the next step, polishing your writing.

Chapter III
POLISHING YOUR WORK

● ● ● ● ● ● ● ● ● ● ● ● ● ● ●

◆ FINE-TUNING

If you want to make your best impression — and a good grade — you're not finished. Now it's time to review and polish your work. Look for things you may have missed when you were concentrating on organizing your ideas. Your excellent thoughts have to be presented in a way that makes sense to others. You can do this by using good grammar, punctuating clearly, spelling correctly, and editing critically.

Good grammar makes a good impression.

The basis for clear writing is good grammar. These are the rules by which everyone is guided — like rules in a soccer game. Although grammar changes slightly across the English-speaking world, there are standards for American English that you need to learn. Grammar helps you communicate your thoughts clearly. Incorrect grammar is a distraction. You impress others by showing that you know the rules and can follow them.

CHECK THE GRAMMAR OF THE SENTENCE.
• • • • • • • • • • • • • • • • •

✏ **SUBJECT AND VERB AGREE IN NUMBER.**

The subject tells who or what the sentence is about. The verb, or predicate, tells what it is that the subject is doing or being. The subject and verb pair up to form the core of the sentence. Both must be singular, or both must be plural.

✏ **NUMBER TELLS YOU HOW MANY PEOPLE OR THINGS YOU ARE WRITING ABOUT.**

One thing is **singular.** Two or more things are **plural.** Put singular subjects with singular verbs and plural subjects with plural verbs.

Examples:

> George Washington and John Adams **were** the first elected leaders of the United States.

> Washington **was** the President. Adams **was** the Vice President.

There are many stumbling blocks to subject–verb agreement.

The intervening phrase

Sometimes a phrase appears between the subject and verb and causes confusion about whether to use a singular or plural verb. For example:

Wrong: One of the boys **are** missing.

Right: One of the boys **is** missing.

The subject of the above sentence is **one** (singular), and the correct verb is **is** (singular). The sentence grows like this:

One is.

One is missing.

One of the boys is missing.

Of the boys is useful information, but **boys** is not the subject. It is the object of the preposition **of.**

Try to see the sentence without the phrase, and the subject and verb agreement will be easier.

Indefinite pronouns

Everybody, anybody, either, neither, each, and **any** are indefinite pronouns. They are all singular and take a singular verb. When they are used as the subject of a sentence, an intervening phrase between them and the verb often makes it difficult to choose the right verb.

Wrong: Neither of the answers **are** good.

Right: Neither of the answers **is** good.

Think of the sentence this way:

Neither is.

Neither is good.

Neither of the answers **is good.**

Wrong: Each of us **have** a chance to win.

Right: Each of us **has** a chance to win.

Each has.

Each has a chance to win.

Each of us has a chance to win.

To make sure that the subject and verb agree, test them side by side without the rest of the sentence. This eliminates the confusion caused by other words in the sentence.

More than one subject

When there is more than one subject, decide the correct form of the verb by thinking of a pronoun that could be used for the subjects, such as:

Wrong: Katie and I **am** very tall.

Right: Katie and I (we) **are** very tall.

Wrong: Ben and Oliver **loves** ice cream.

Right: Ben and Oliver (they) **love** ice cream.

Collective nouns

Use a singular verb when the subject sounds plural but refers only to one thing. For example:

Barnum and Bailey (the circus) **is** my favorite circus.

Strawberries and cream (a dessert) **was** Tamika's favorite breakfast.

Sentences introduced by **there**

To make the subject and verb agree in number, find out what the real subject is. When the adverb **there** is used as an introductory word in a sentence, it is frequently mistaken for the subject.

Example:

Wrong: **There was** one test tube and one Bunsen burner in the lab.

Subject: **one** test tube and **one** Bunsen burner

Right: **There were** one test tube and one Bunsen burner in the lab.

Questions

In a question, the subject follows the verb. If this makes the subject difficult to find, put the question back into statement form. The subject and verb will then be more obvious.

Wrong: **Is** a basketball and a football the same price?

Reverse: A basketball and a football (they) **are** the same price.

Right: **Are** a basketball and a football the same price?

✏ **PICK THE RIGHT PRONOUN FOR THE JOB.**

You can get by with the wrong pronouns in everyday speech because you know that people will probably understand you anyway. For example:

Me and him caught a frog.

They understand it, but you know that it isn't correct. The reason is that different pronouns do different jobs. Many people confuse subject, object, and possessive pronouns. If you know a pronoun's job in a sentence, you will know which one to use.

Subject pronouns

The pronouns that do things are **I, we, you, he, she, it, they, who,** and **whoever.** They are subject pronouns. For example:

> **Whoever** said that **he** and **she** were going to win was right.

Compound subjects of a sentence

Compound subjects with one or more pronouns cause a great deal of trouble. If you are having difficulty with combinations of pronouns, try them one at a time.

> **Sentence: Me** and **her** went to the movies.

> **Sounds wrong: Me** went to the movies.
>
> **Her** went to the movies.

> **Sounds right:** **I** went to the movies.
>
> **She** went to the movies.

> **Correct: She** and **I** went to the movies.

When the compound subject of a sentence has both a noun and a pronoun, you can tell which form of the pronoun to use by trying it alone.

Sentence: Jamie and **me** ate popcorn.

Sounds wrong: Me ate popcorn.

Sounds right: I ate popcorn.

Correct: Jamie and **I** ate popcorn.

With verbs of being

Verbs of "to be" call for a balancing act with pronouns. The verbs of being are **be, am, is, are, was, were, been.** These verbs do not have objects. They must be used with subject pronouns.

Sentences with these verbs are always balanced and can be reversed and still mean the same thing. Therefore, a pronoun following one of these verbs has to be a subject pronoun since it could easily be put in front of the verb and become the subject.

Incorrect: It was **her.**

If we reverse the sentence:

Sounds wrong: Her was it.

Sounds right: She was it.

Correct: It was **she.**

Incorrect: The boy calling could be **him.**

Reverse the sentence:

Wrong: Him could be the boy calling.

Right: He could be the boy calling.

Correct: The boy calling could be **he.**

Incorrect: It must have been **her** and **him.**

Reverse and separate the pronouns:

Sounds wrong: Her must have been it.

Him must have been it.

Sounds right: She must have been it.

He must have been it.

Correct: It must have been **she** and **he.**

Always use a subject pronoun with a being verb.

Object pronouns

The pronouns that receive, rather than initiate, action are **me, us, you, him, her, it, them, whom**, and **whomever**. For example:

> The sergeant ordered **her** to tell **them** that they should follow **him.**

As compound objects of a verb

When two pronouns are the object of a verb, they should both be object pronouns. To test which pronoun to use, try them separately.

> **Sentence:** The dog bit **he** and **I.**
>
> **Sounds wrong:** The dog bit **he.**
>
> The dog bit **I.**
>
> **Sounds right:** The dog bit **him.**
>
> The dog bit **me.**
>
> **Correct:** The dog bit **him** and **me.**

As the object of a preposition

Prepositions are words such as **about, after, beside, between, for, from, of, to,** and **with** that connect words and phrases to the rest of the sentence. They are followed by an object pronoun.

When using two pronouns together after a preposition, some people think it sounds better to use the subject pronoun. They think it sounds more educated. Actually, it is just the opposite. You can hear how incorrect it is by trying one pronoun at a time.

Sentence: The class voted for **he** and **I.**

Sounds wrong: The class voted for **he.**

The class voted for **I.**

Sounds right: The class voted for **him.**

The class voted for **me.**

Correct: The class voted for **him** and **me.**

As compound objects of a preposition

The same error occurs when a noun and a pronoun follow the preposition. Here again, try the pronoun by itself.

Sentence: The teacher walked beside Cara and **I.**

Sounds wrong: The teacher walked beside **I.**

Sounds right: The teacher walked beside **me.**

Correct: The teacher walked beside Cara and **me.**

PUNCTUATION HOLDS IT ALL TOGETHER.

Punctuation tells the reader how you want your words to be read. When you speak, your voice puts in many of these punctuation marks.

At the end of a sentence, you take a breath.

(You've just put in a period.)

When you ask a question, you raise your voice at the end.

(Does the listener hear a question mark?)

When you want to emphasize something, you say it louder.

(This is a doggone exclamation mark!)

When you pause during a sentence, you are deliberately separating certain words for clearer meaning.

(You, my friend, have just used a comma.)

When people are reading what you wrote, they have nothing to go by except the words they see on the paper. Punctuation takes the place of your voice.

✏ SENTENCES HAVE TO BEGIN AND END.

A sentence is a group of words that tell a complete thought. You signal the beginning of a sentence by capitalizing the first word and following the last word with a period, question mark, or exclamation mark. You can't expect the reader to know when you have finished one thought and gone on to another unless you mark each sentence.

If you wrote a paragraph without punctuating, it might look like this:

> Every summer we go to a great
> camp in the mountains we go swimming
> sailing and fishing in the lake the
> first day of our vacation last summer
> I caught a huge trout reeling it in
> was exhausting and exciting I will
> never forget that day or the fish
> fry that followed.

Without punctuation, the reader sees a jumble of words. With punctuation, it looks like this:

> Every summer we go to a great
> camp in the mountains. We go
> swimming, sailing, and fishing in the
> lake. The first day of our vacation

*last summer I caught a huge trout.
Reeling it in was exhausting and
exciting. I will never forget that day
or the fish fry that followed.*

The reader has to be signaled about stops and pauses in order to understand the words.

✏ **COMMAS SEPARATE CERTAIN WORDS AND PHRASES FROM THE REST OF THE SENTENCE.**

When you speak, you group some words together and separate others within each sentence. You do this to be understood better. In writing, the comma makes these pauses for you. Here are some examples of comma uses.

Words in a series

Commas are so important to words in a series that by simply changing their location, the whole meaning of the sentence changes.

Example One:

Please go to the store and buy ice, cream, vanilla, pudding, and chocolate cake.

Example Two:

> Please go to the store and buy ice cream, vanilla
> pudding, and chocolate cake.

In Example One you have to buy five items. In Example Two you have to buy three items. The comma divides the words at exactly the place you would have to pause to make the meaning clear.

In the following sentence, all commas are omitted.

> Bobby Earl Michael James and Eddie went to the park.

You don't know how many boys there were. It depends on where you place the commas. In the following sentence, there were three boys.

> Bobby Earl, Michael James, and Eddie went to
> the park.

Note: Sometimes the comma is omitted in front of the "and" before the final word or phrase of a series. It is best to put in the final comma to be certain that the reader understands the separation of the last two items.

Words in a series can be written with no commas by using a connecting word (and, or, nor) between each listing to show the separation.

Example:

Bobby Earl **and** Michael **and** James **and** Eddie went to the park.

(Four boys went.)

Descriptive phrase (appositive)

Use commas to set off words and phrases that are descriptive but not absolutely necessary to the sentence meaning. If you read the following examples out loud, you can hear the pauses that the commas represent.

Example:

My dad's car**, an old clunker,** broke down on the way home.

This sentence meaning is the same if you say: My dad's car broke down on the way home. "An old clunker" is put in for added but not necessary information.

Caution: When a descriptive phrase is necessary to the sentence, it is not set off by commas. You do not pause in speaking when you use a phrase of this kind.

Right: The man **in the boat** waved at me.

Wrong: The man**, in the boat,** waved at me.

It was not just any man who waved at me. It was the man in the boat. This is not set off by commas because it is necessary to the meaning of the sentence.

Parenthetical expressions

Use commas to set off words thrown into sentences as a casual comment. In speaking, you pause before and after these parenthetical expressions. They don't change the meaning of the sentence and could be left out.

Examples:

My dog**, of course,** is the best trained.

To tell the truth, I forgot to do my homework.

Samantha**, I suppose,** is the best singer.

Clauses — independent and dependent

A clause has a subject and a verb just like a sentence. A clause that can stand by itself as a sentence is called an **independent clause.** A **dependent clause** is a sentence beginning with a word that makes it dependent on the rest of the sentence. For example:

I am going to tell you about *The Giver*

(an independent clause)

because it is the best book I've read this year.

(dependent clause)

Introductory dependent clause

The introductory dependent clause sets the scene for the rest of the sentence. Follow it with a comma when writing, just as you would follow it with a pause when speaking. (If you left out the first word of the introductory clause in the following examples, you would have a complete sentence and, therefore, would have to use a comma and a conjunction to connect it to the second part.)

Examples:

> **Because faking it did not work,** Gino was forced to study.

> **If I like a book,** I read it very slowly.

Introductory phrase

A comma is used after an introductory phrase if you think the reader would otherwise be confused or if the phrase is especially long.

Example (no comma because of short length):

> **Briefly** the plot goes like this.

Example (with a comma because of long length):

> **In the early morning hours in January,** there was an earthquake in California.

Example (with a comma for clarity):

> **In short,** people are funny.

✏ ## APOSTROPHES HAVE A TRIPLE JOB.

To show possession

Imagine the phrase "belonging to" when showing that one thing belongs to another. Place the apostrophe and an "s" right after the last word of that phrase.

Examples:

> The book belonging to Jessica was found on the playground.
>
> **Jessica's** book was found on the playground.

> The bicycle belonging to Charles is on the front porch.
>
> **Charles's** bicycle is on the front porch.

In the following sentence, the phrase is "belonging to the men." The apostrophe goes right after the last word of that phrase. That word is "men."

Example:

> The voices belonging to the men grew louder.
>
> The **men's** voices grew louder.

When a noun is plural and ends in **s** already, simply add an apostrophe to show possession.

> The house belonging to the Browns is for sale.
>
> The **Browns'** house is for sale.

To form contractions

A contraction is a word in which letters have been left out and two words have been put together. Signal the missing letter or letters by putting in an apostrophe where the letters would have been.

Examples:

> **don't** (do not)
>
> **he's** (he is)
>
> **they've** (they have)
>
> **you're** (you are)

In writing dialogue, you may also use the apostrophe to show letters that weren't actually pronounced.

Example:

> "He loves **singin'** and **dancin'**," she said.
> *(He loves singing and dancing.)*

To make special words plural

An apostrophe is used to show the plural of numbers, signs, and letters of the alphabet.

Example:

> I don't want to hear any more **if's, and's,** or **but's** from you.

Note: Apostrophes are never used for the plurals of other words. The apostrophe is used to form plurals only for numbers, special emblems, individual letters, and words being referred to as words.

Examples:

> **Wrong:** The **Christopher's** wish you a Happy New Year.

> **Right:** The **Christophers** wish you a Happy New Year.

> **Wrong:** **Birthday's** are special.

> **Right:** **Birthdays** are special.

✏ **QUOTATION MARKS IDENTIFY SPOKEN AND BORROWED WORDS.**

To show spoken words

Use quotation marks for all written reporting of conversation whether it is real or imaginary. If someone is supposed to be speaking, the words are enclosed in quotation marks.

Examples:

Tommy saw the dog coming and yelled, **"Let's get out of here!"**

"Are you positive," asked the hairdresser, **"that you want your hair green?"**

Only the words actually spoken are put within the quotation marks. Other words are left outside and are separated from the quote by a comma.

Final punctuation that would have been used with the original words is left inside the quotation marks. Final punctuation that is not part of the quotation is put outside the quotation marks. In the following example, the sentence is a question, but the quote is not. This time, the question mark goes outside the quotes.

Did you hear him say, "I don't want to go"?

Note: A sentence can have only one ending punctuation mark — never two.

To quote written words

When you use someone else's words from a book or letter, show the reader that the words are not your own. (See page 44 for more information about this.) Short quotes are written with quotation marks around them.

Example:

> **"Let them eat cake!"** Marie Antoinette is said to have remarked when told the French peasants had no bread.

Long quotes can be shown with the words centered, single-spaced, and indented on both sides.

Example:

Here is the account of Eugenia Zieber who was eighteen years old when she made the overland trip from Illinois to Oregon in 1851. Her entire family had boarded a covered wagon and set out for a new life. On the Fourth of July, 1851, she wrote in her diary:

> July 4. The cattle had a stampede
> to day. The only thing nearby that
> was done in the way of celebrating
> the fourth. The stampede was
> started by dog's jumping out suddenly
> from under one of the wagons No harm

done. I must not forget that the young
men marched round the camp this
evening after supper, whistling Yank
Doodle. Mrs. Bowman, Brown, mother
and I caught up some tin pans and
sticks and started after, but backed
out. Could not go quite so far . . .

The quotation must be exact — even with punctuation and spelling errors. If you do not use some of the quote, indicate that by putting in three periods (. . .). If the deleted passage comes at the end of a sentence, add a fourth period. When handwriting quotation marks, make sure that the beginning marks face toward the sentence and the ending marks face backwards, toward the sentence. This helps the reader's eye identify the speaker or the quoted passage.

Note: Be sure to include in your bibliography the names of the books from which you take long quotations. (See page 126.)

STANDARD SPELLING MAKES IT READABLE.

Words are spelled the way they are because that spelling is traditional and is understandable to most Americans. Standard spelling assures the reader that your words can be trusted. Every day, however, we see words that have a shorthand or unconventional spelling.

Examples:

Ped Xing . . . . pedestrian crossing

no thru way . . . . . not a through way

Xmas . . . . Christmas

OK . . . . okay

4 Sale . . . . for sale

Usually these words have been shortened because the abbreviated version takes up less space. Even though you understand these words, they should not be used in formal writing. Don't be tempted to take shortcuts.

When you read a book published in Canada or England, the spelling may be different. The same is true of books published a long time ago in the United States. If you don't know the modern American spelling for a word, look it up in a dictionary or run it through your computer spell check.

WATCH FOR CONFUSING WORDS AND PHRASES.

There are rules about the use of all words and phrases. Sometimes people either don't know these rules or they choose to ignore them. When words are misused over and over, often the wrong forms are so common that they become more and more acceptable — especially in everyday speech.

When writing, however, you need to know what is correct. Words that you misuse in talking with friends may look sloppy on paper.

Following are a few of the most commonly misused words. They are divided into four sections: **Verbs, Prepositions, Adjectives and Adverbs,** and **Pronouns.**

✏ SOME VERBS ARE TRICKY.

Verbs are words that show action or a state of being. There are regular and irregular verbs. When learning to talk, small children usually make all verbs regular. They will say:

He **throwed** the ball.

My bike **runned** into the curb.

Uncle Jack **catched** my cold.

This pattern is certainly logical if all verbs were regular. With correction and experience, however, we learn that there are some verbs with irregular forms.

He **threw** the ball.

My bike **ran** into the curb.

Uncle Jack **caught** my cold.

(For more information about regular and irregular verbs, see the Scholastic Guide *Checking Your Grammar.*)

The following verbs listed in this section are confusing for other reasons than that they are irregular.

affect – effect

These two words sound enough alike that you can say either one when talking, and the listener will know what you mean. In writing, however, you must choose one or the other because, depending on how they are spelled, they mean different things.

Affect means to impress or to influence.

Effect means to bring something about.

Examples:

> The noise outside **affects** (influences) how well I do my homework.

> Stirring pudding **effects** (brings about) a smoother, yummier dessert.

Note: The word **effect** *may also be used as a noun meaning the result of what was brought about.*

Example:

> That bump on the head had no **effect** on me on me on me.

can – may

These two verbs are often used interchangeably. Although the listener seldom has trouble figuring out what is meant, you should use them precisely when you write.

Can means to be able.

May means to have permission.

Examples:

> **May** I climb that mountain?
>
> *(Do I have permission?)*

> **Can** I climb that mountain?
>
> *(Am I able?)*

could of – would of

These forms are incorrect. They began as *could have* and *would have*, shortened to the contractions *could've* and *would've*, which sounded like *could of* and *would of*. When writing, it is important to use the correct form.

Example:

> **Wrong:** He **could of** done it.

> **Right:** He **could have** done it.

or

He **could've** done it.

goes – says

We often hear people say something like this:

I **go,** "Are you sure?" and he **goes,** "Sure," and I **go,** "Cool."

To go has many meanings, but it should not be substituted for *to say* or *to ask* or *to reply* or *to answer*. Instead, write

I **asked,** "Are you sure?" and he **replied** "Sure."
I **said,** "Cool."

Bonus: Here are some acceptable substitutions for **said.**

replied	whispered	answered
asked	commented	inquired
shouted	murmured	demanded

hung – hanged

The verb **to hang** means to suspend (something). It has two past tense forms: **hung** and **hanged.**

Hung means suspended.

Hanged means suspended by the neck until dead.

Examples:

> The portrait was **hung** in the White House.

> John Brown was **hanged** for starting a slave revolt.

lay – lie

The verb **to lay** has three parts: **lay, laid, laid.**

To lay means to put something someplace. It requires an object.

Examples:

> **Present tense: Lay** your napkin on your lap.

> **Past tense:** He **laid** his napkin on a chair.

> **Past participle:** He had **laid** the napkin there yesterday.

To lie has two meanings. One is to make a false statement.

Example:

> To **lie** under oath is perjury.

The three parts of this verb are: **lie, lied, lied.**

Examples:

> **Present tense:** The first witness **lies.**

Past tense: The second witness said he **lied.**

Past participle: The third witness said that earlier witnesses had **lied.**

To lie may also mean to rest or recline.

Example:

The dog is not supposed to **lie** on my bed.

This meaning has slightly different parts: **lie, lay, lain.**

Examples:

Present tense: I **lie** down every day at two o'clock.

Past tense: Yesterday I forgot to **lay** down.

Past participle: Now I wish I had **lain** down all afternoon.

sit – set

These verbs are often confused, probably because they sound so much alike. However, they have quite different meanings.

To **sit** means to be seated.

To **set** means to put something someplace.

Examples:

> Aunt Polly told Tom Sawyer to **sit** down.
>
> First he **set** his bucket on the steps.
>
> **To set** can also mean to firm up. Pudding and bones can **set.**

wait on – wait for

To wait on means to serve someone.

Example:

> He **waited** on our table first.

To **wait for** means to stay put until something expected happens.

Example:

> John **waited for** Teresa to come.
>
> *(John stayed put expecting Teresa to come.)*

Note: Remember that at restaurants you wait **for** *someone to wait* **on** *you.*

✐ PREPOSITIONS MAKE THE RIGHT CONNECTIONS.

Prepositions are words that connect ideas. There are about fifty prepositions in everyday use. The following are some that are frequently misused.

about – at about

About is sufficient by itself. **At about** is unnecessary.

Too wordy: We will eat **at about** one o'clock.

Better: We will eat **about** one o'clock.

among – between

Today **between** is used more often than **among.** The distinction between the two words is fading fast. However, there is a difference.

Between is a preposition used when there are two people, two things, or two groups.

Example:

Draw a line **between** the two points.

Among is a preposition meant to be used when there are more than two of something.

Example:

Choose one figure from **among** the triangle, the quadrangle, the circle, and the hexagon.

like – as

Like is a preposition that is followed by a phrase.

Example:

She snorts **like** a horse.

As is a conjunction. It introduces clauses with a subject and a verb.

Example:

Do **as** I do and not **as** I say.

in – into

In means inside something.

Into means moving toward something or moving inside it. Compare the following:

Jack's pet canary flew **in** the house.

Jack's pet canary flew **into** the house. (Ouch!)

✏ ADJECTIVES AND ADVERBS SHOULD BE PRECISE.

An adjective describes a noun or pronoun; an adverb describes a verb, adjective, or other adverb.

Example:

The **unhappy** dog is barking **loudly.**

Unhappy is an adjective describing dog (a noun).

Loudly is an adverb describing barking (a verb).

Here are a few adjectives and adverbs that cause confusion.

anyway – anyways

The adverb **anyway** means in any case, anyhow. **Anyway** does not have a plural form. Therefore, **anyways** is never correct.

> **Wrong:** That's not the theme of the story **anyways.**

> **Right:** That's not the theme of the story **anyway.**

bad – badly

These two words are often confused. **Bad** is an adjective; **badly** is an adverb.

With parts of the verb **to be** — **be, am, is, are, was, were, been** — and with verbs relating to the senses: **seem, look, feel, taste, sound,** and **smell** — use the adjective **bad.**

Example:

All the reviews of this movie were **bad.**

With an action verb, use the adverb **badly.**

Example:

> He left the cast of the play because he was performing **badly.**

farther – further

Farther refers to a longer distance.

Further refers to a longer time or a greater amount.

Examples:

> Our team moved the ball **farther** in the first quarter.

> We discussed the game **further** in the locker room.

fewer – less

Both **fewer** and **less** are used for comparisons. The difference is as follows:

Fewer refers to a smaller number of things.

Less refers to a smaller portion of one thing.

Examples:

> We have **fewer** assignments on weekends than on weekdays.

We have **less** homework on weekends than on weekdays.

healthy – healthful

These two adjectives are used interchangeably, but there is a difference.

Healthy means to have good health.

Healthful means to give good health.

Examples:

Regular exercise is **healthful.**

To be **healthy,** exercise regularly.

most – almost

It is common to hear **almost** shortened to **most.** There is a difference.

Most means the greatest amount.

Almost means nearly.

Examples:

Most cultures showed mold.

Almost all of the cultures showed mold.

off – off of

Although you may hear **off of** a great deal, the **of** is unnecessary. **Off** is fine by itself.

> **Unnecessary:** Pablo risks his life by jumping **off of** a roof.

> **Better:** Pablo risks his life by jumping **off** a roof.

real – really

Real is often used when **really** is what is meant. They are different in meaning.

Real is an adjective that means true or actual.

Really is an adverb that means extremely.

Examples:

> A **real** story is often stranger than fiction.

> What happened to him is **really** frightening.

> You need an adverb to describe the adjective **frightening.**

✏ **SUBSTITUTE PRONOUNS WITH CARE.**

Pronouns take the place of nouns. Confusion often results from not understanding which nouns they replace.

each other – one another

These words are used interchangeably. To be exact, however, **each other** refers to two people, and **one another** refers to three or more.

Examples:

Jerry and Cameron took turns questioning **each other.**

The team members shared ideas with **one another.**

himself – herself – themselves

Pronouns that end in **self**— myself, yourself, himself, herself, ourselves, yourselves, themselves — must match the noun or pronoun they make stronger or reflect.

Examples:

The queen **herself** never married.

When the battle was done, the knight and his squire congratulated **themselves.**

Hisself and **theirselves** are not words. They should never be used instead of **himself** and **themselves.**

Pronouns ending in **self** cannot be the subject of a sentence. **Myself** cannot be used instead of **I** .

Examples:

> **Wrong:** The teacher and **myself** were alone in the room.

> **Right:** The teacher and **I** were alone in the room.

its – it's

These words sound exactly alike, so they don't present a problem when you are speaking. When writing, however, you must differentiate.

Its is a possessive pronoun. Even though it shows possession, it does not have an apostrophe.

Example:

> My snake lost **its** skin.

It's is the contraction for **it is.** The apostrophe shows that the **i** is left out of the word **is**

Example:

> I don't care if **it's** (it is) late.

who – that

Current usage is as follows:

Who refers to people.

> The blond girl is the one **who** spoke.

That may refer to both people and things.

It was the dripping faucet **that** drove him crazy.

The blond girl was the one **that** spoke.

who – whom

Who is a subject pronoun. **Whom** is an object pronoun. To help determine which one to use, do the following:

Substitute the subject pronoun **he** or **she** for **who.**

Substitute the object pronoun **him** or **her** for **whom.**

Example:

Who or **whom** was yelling?

Substituting the words **he** and **him,** would you say:

He was yelling?

or

Him was yelling?

Obviously, you would choose the word **he** Therefore, the sentence would be:

Who was yelling?

Example:

I don't care **who** said it.

or

I don't care **whom** said it.

You would say: **He** said it. Therefore, the correct sentence is:

I don't care **who** said it.

Example:

I don't know **whom** to tell.

or

I don't know **who** to tell.

You would say: Tell **him.** Therefore, the correct sentence is:

I don't know **whom** to tell.

EDITING MAKES IT SHINE.
• • • • • • • • • • • • • • • •

You may have heard that you never get a second chance to make a good first impression. That may be true with many things but not with writing. When you speak, your words jump out of your mouth and are gone. When you write, you have a second chance. You can even have third and fourth chances if you want them. Be sure you leave enough time to go over your work and make changes before you turn it in. Reviewing and changing what you have written is a valuable tool in developing writing style.

✏ THIS ONE'S FOR YOUR EYES ONLY.

Read your first draft straight through from beginning to end with the knowledge that you're going to rewrite and improve it. As you read it a second and even a third time, look at your words from the reader's point of view. Ask yourself:

- ◆ How do these words sound? Is the emphasis where I want it?
- ◆ Would a different word make the idea clearer?
- ◆ Am I repeating a certain word too much?
- ◆ Does the punctuation make it clear where to stop, to begin, to pause?

✏ LITTLE THINGS MEAN A LOT.

As you read what you wrote, you will see ways to improve it. These may include:

- ◆ Substituting a better word here and there
- ◆ Adding a word that may have been left out

- Crossing out unnecessary words

- Removing unneeded sentences

- Rewriting a sentence

- Combining paragraphs or dividing a paragraph

- Adding information or deleting off-target information

- Improving punctuation

- Changing paragraph order

✏ IT'S NOT IN STONE.

Lots of writers like to think their first draft is their best. They are usually mistaken — or lazy. The best writers fine-tune their work long after the initial inspiration has passed. You may want to reshuffle pages or even cut them up and tape them together in new ways. Try reading to a friend or parent or, if you're by yourself, simply read aloud. If you read every word, you may be surprised by what you hear.

✏ COMPUTERS ARE WONDERFUL — UP TO A POINT.

If you are using a word processor, it probably has many tools to help you edit.

Deleting

You can delete a word or phrase with a stroke of the keyboard, but ask yourself: Did I really want to delete those words? Did I delete only the words I meant to? Does deleting these words change the grammar of the sentence? Does it require me to change other words in the sentence?

Spell checking

It's often easy to misspell a word — even if you know how to spell it — in the rush to get your ideas into words. You should *never* turn in an assignment without running a spell check if you have one. But computers are machines. A spell check cannot detect a misspelled word if the spelling is correct for another word.

Example:

The nights eight and drank at there fast.

What your probably meant to write was:

The knights ate and drank at their feast.

The spell checker can't distinguish between **nights** and **knights, eight** and **ate,** and **there** and **their,** and **fast** and **feast** — as long as each is spelled correctly.

Proper nouns present problems for most spell checkers, too. Not surprisingly, your computer will probably be stymied by Syracuse or Dred Scott. Some spell checkers have a feature that allows you to add words to your dictionary, so you may want to add proper nouns that you use frequently — after you check your dictionary or source to make sure you've spelled them correctly.

Moving text

Have you ever wondered how a piece of work would read if you put the last paragraph first or exchanged two sentences? With a word processor, this is a simple procedure. However, once you have moved the text and saved it, be sure you read your draft through again. It may not read as clearly as you expected. That is why Undo is a favorite command of many writers.

Grammar check

More recent word-processing programs have features that allow you to check basic grammar, such as subject-verb agreement and punctuation. A feature like this can be useful if you use it carefully. But make sure that you didn't punctuate oddly for effect, or bad grammar has not been used intentionally.

✏ **THE FINAL DRAFT IS DONE.**

Here is an example of a paragraph that was written, then reread and changed, and then put in final form:

First Draft

My grandmother is really nice to me, but she has to be really, really old. I mean, she is my mother's mother, and my mother is ancient. But when I am with my grandmother, we always have a good time. We do neat things like play the piano, go for walks, talk about how great I am, buy me presents, cook my favorite foods, and play games that I win. Maybe being really, really old isn't so bad when you have a really neat granddaughter like me.

Second Draft with changes and corrections:

My grandmother is very nice, but she has to be really old. After all, she is my mother's mother, and my mother's ancient. When I'm with her, however, I always have a good time. We play the piano, go for walks, talk about how wonderful I am, buy me presents, cook my favorite foods, and play games that I always win. Maybe being so old isn't that bad when you have a terrific granddaughter like me.

✏ **HARD WORK PAYS OFF.**

The advantage of reviewing and changing your work is that the finished product more closely says what you want. The final product shows none of these revisions. Because the material has been reviewed and revised, it reads more smoothly, is easier to understand, and reflects your thoughts more accurately. To the rest of the world, your final draft might well be your first draft. Only you know for sure.

Chapter IV
PRESENTING YOUR WORK
• • • • • • • • • • • • • • •

◆ YOUR BEST PAPER FORWARD

Congratulations — you're finished! Well, almost finished. You can do a fine job of planning, producing, and polishing your work and still make a bad impression on the reader if your presentation is sloppy.

Readers react not only to what is written but also to how it looks. A report, no matter how brilliant, must look as good as it really is.

> If you want an A-plus, it must look like an A-plus paper.

Always make sure your paper is clean — no cola stains or ragged edges — and well labeled. You're not one of those people who forgets to include your name on the front page, are you?

The style of your presentation may vary. However, just as there are basics for writing well, there are basics for ensuring that material will make a positive impression under any conditions.

BY HAND OR MACHINE?
• • • • • • • • • • • • • • • • •

By now, you know how you will create your final draft. Will you write it, type it, or use a word processor? Each has its own rules.

✎ HANDWRITING CAN BE IMPRESSIVE.

Although few people make the effort to present them well anymore, handwritten reports can be elegant, impressive, and an expression of the writer's creativity. Start with a pen with plenty of ink. Blue-black is the most readable on white paper.

Find a smooth, uncluttered surface and give yourself time to write legibly. Select fresh, unwrinkled paper with clean edges. Before you begin, decide where you will put your margins — on the right and left and top and bottom — and stick with them. The lines can help guide you.

A little white correction fluid is permissible, but if you use it, make sure you let it dry before you write over it. If you make a lot of mistakes, it's better to start a new page.

Since your final draft has been carefully edited, stick to it.

✏ TYPEWRITERS STILL WORK.

Perhaps your handwriting is not so great, and you're unable to use a word processor. You can do as people did for several generations, and use a typewriter.

Typewriters have fewer features than word processors, and most don't have any memory in which to store your work. However, they do have uniform characters and can help you create a crisp, well-crafted manuscript.

Make sure you have sufficient paper with no lines or holes as well as some correction fluid for the occasional mistake.

When you type, you must make sure you strike the keys evenly so that they don't create a jagged line or uneven spacing.

Here is part of a sentence typed badly:

```
Ipledg e allegancet
othe flagof the uniPed sttes
o  famerica.
```

In typing, the problem is how you put the letters together. If you type the wrong letter, put a space in the wrong place, leave out a letter, or put in an extra letter, the words are unreadable.

Properly typed, the sentence above reads:

```
I pledge allegiance to the
flag of the United States of
America . . .
```

Accurately typed words please the reader and show that you have pride and confidence in what you have written.

✎ WORD PROCESSORS ARE NIFTY.

If you use a word processor, no one has to tell you how handy it is for writing and rewriting. You may have already saved several versions of your writing. Now you can create your final paper without much effort.

Not so fast! In spite of the ease with which word processors make it possible for writers to create and save their work, some of the sloppiest presentations are electronically created. Why is this? Perhaps it's because people expect the machines to do all the work. No matter how powerful your computer, you, the writer, are in command. And if you skip some steps along the way, don't be surprised if your grades reflect it.

No computer can save you if you fail to use the special features of your word processor to create even margins, tabs, and spacing. It's up to you to enter the words carefully and to reread what you write.

Special print features

When you handwrite a report, you learn to underline words that should be in italics or boldface. Word processors can help you by actually creating italics and boldface type. Make sure you use these features consistently, not italicizing some titles and underlining others.

Most word processors give you a choice of print faces and sizes. If you are creating a manuscript in which there are examples or mathematical equations, these special features can help you lead the reader through your work.

When used wisely, a word processor and printer can help you look like a professional publisher. When used carelessly, they create the wrong impression.

PRESENTATION MAKES IT NEAT.

✐ FORMAT UNIFORMLY.

The way you present your paper is called its format. It is the form you give your paper. For instance, the first time you indent a paragraph, you announce that this is how all paragraphs will be done.

Just as you are frustrated when playing a game with someone who changes the rules all the time, so readers are frustrated if you suddenly change your format. When you start writing, you are saying to the reader, "This is the way I'm going to do this." If you do something else, you have changed the rules. Be consistent.

Here are examples of common format decisions you should make:

1. How big will your margins be? On either side? At top and bottom?

2. Will paragraphs be indented or written in block form with extra space between paragraphs?

3. How will you treat titles, headings, subheadings?

4. Will you use abbreviations? If you do, be sure to abbreviate the same way every time. (For example, Atlanta, GA every time — never Atlanta, Georgia, then Atlanta, GA)

5. Will you spell out numbers over 100? (You should always write out numbers under 100.)

6. Will you hyphenate words when they don't fit on a single line, or will you move the entire word to the next line?

7. Will you use titles with people's names? (Mr., Miss, Ms., or Mrs. Johnson, for example.)

8. Will you use first names? Nicknames? Middle initials?

To a reader, a predictable, orderly format is like a security blanket.

✏ USE SPACING TO ORGANIZE YOUR WORK.

Well-spaced writing is easier to read and to understand. It looks organized. Here are some spacing suggestions that will improve your final presentation:

1. Leave uniform space at the top and bottom of the page.

2. Allow for a left and right margin of about one inch on each page.

3. Keep the left margin straight and the right margin as uniform as possible.

4. Allow extra space between paragraphs.

5. Leave space above and below titles and headings.

6. Double-space typed text.

7. Give special attention to lines of poetry; spacing is often part of the poem.

8. In scripts, lines of dialogue are often single-spaced with double-spacing between the speakers.

9. Indent quoted passages from other works on both sides. These passages may be single-spaced.

10. Use only one side of the paper unless instructed to do otherwise.

Spacing not only improves the look of your writing, it also makes it easier to read and, therefore, to understand.

✐ ORGANIZE BY NUMBERING.

Pages

One of the most important ways to help readers is by numbering the pages. Anything over one page of writing should be numbered at the top center, the bottom, or the top right of each page. The numbers should appear in the same place on every page. By numbering the pages, you make it easier to find a certain page and to keep them in order. Some writers do not number the first page. If you follow this style, be sure the second page is numbered "2."

Sections

Divide your long works into sections and number them. If you use an outline to create a report, the Roman numeral headings often give you clues for section headings. If you write a long work of fiction, you may want to divide it into numbered chapters. Plays may be numbered by acts and scenes. (See page 68.)

✐ THE TABLE OF CONTENTS GOES UP FRONT.

At the front of a long work, include a table of contents. Be sure to include the titles, your introduction, the bibliography, and any illustrations — and the number of the page on which each can be found.

BIBLIOGRAPHIES BACK IT UP.

● ● ● ● ● ● ● ● ● ● ● ● ● ● ●

When you began taking notes for your report or essay, you took careful notes about where you got your information, didn't you? (If you didn't, there's still time to return to the library.) All this material can now be organized at the back of your paper. Although your teacher may tell you to vary your format, here are some suggestions.

Here is the way you would list the source for Eugenia's diary entry (see page 93) in your bibliography.

Holmes, Kenneth L., editor, *Covered Wagon Women,*
Vol. III, Arthur H. Clarke Co., Glendale, CA, 1984.

Notice that the name of the editor (or author) comes first, but it is listed by last name first. The title of the book comes next, the number of the volume (Most books, of course, have only one volume, so often you can skip that), followed by the name of the publisher, the city where it was published, and the date of the latest copyright. Notice how the top line hangs out, and the second line is indented. This helps the reader to find each source.

List each source alphabetically, by name. For example, a book by Jean Fritz (Fritz, Jean) would be listed before the Holmes book, and a book by Milton Meltzer (Meltzer, Milton) would come after.

When a book has more than one author

If a book is written by more than one person, begin your entry with the first name on the title page, followed by the second, and a third, if necessary. Each name should be listed last name first, and the entry should be alphabetized by the first author's name.

Books without an author

Suppose you took some information from an encyclopedia. Although encyclopedias have many authors, only the publisher is usually credited in the bibliography.

World Book, 1994, *s.v.* Civil War

(Alphabetize the reference as if the author's name began with W, then list the date of the encyclopedia's copyright, followed by the initials s.v. and the name of the entry quotes.)

Magazine articles

When you quote from a magazine, the entry is still listed under the author's name, followed by the title of the article, the title of the magazine, the volume, number, and date of the magazine, and finally the page number of the article.

Smith, Patricia, "Between Two Worlds," *Scholastic Update,* Vol. 128, No. 11 (March 8, 1996), pp. 12–13.

The Internet

If you use an electronic source, whether it's an online service or a CD-ROM, include that source in your bibliography. If it has an author, list it alphabetically under the author's name. Your entry should include the date of the publication (first, in parentheses) as well as the date when you downloaded the information. The last part of the entry (Available) tells how someone else can find the information.

Smith, John P. "A Very Large Mouse." Children's Literature Journal (1996): Online. Internet. 10 May 1997. Available GOPHER:psts2.xxx.edu

If you use an online or electronic reference work, list the name of the article first.

> "Phonetics." Global Encyclopedia. Online.
>   Internet 4 July 1996. Available
>   http://www.halcyon.com/jensen/encyclopedia/

Other sources

If you interview a person or watch or listen to an interview conducted by someone else, be sure to credit the information in your bibliography.

> Brodkin, Adele, Ph. D., Interview, April 13, 1997.

How to cite sources within your paper is explained in Chapter II, Producing Your Work, pages 44–45.

MAKE THAT FINAL CHECK.
· · · · · · · · · · · · · · · ·

Especially if you rewrote or retyped your final text, read your work out loud. If you can find a partner, this works even better. Reading aloud helps you to catch words that were dropped and words that were repeated. Your partner can also alert you to passages that are unclear or weak.

✏ RECONSIDER YOUR TITLES.

When you started this writing project, you may have had a topic in mind. Maybe your teacher even suggested one. Now that you have written, revised, and polished your work, is the title still appropriate? Or if the topic is essentially the same, would you like for your title to be livelier? Now's your chance to call your work whatever you like. After all, you created it.

If your writing is serious, you need a serious title, but it doesn't have to be dull. *Abigail Adams,* might become, *Abigail Adams, Second First Lady,* or *Abigail Adams, Founding Wife and Mother.* Some writers like mysterious titles: *What I Found at the Mall* or, if you like to play around with sounds, *Mall Mice.* Poets and fiction writers often use single-word titles: *Fragments* or *Censored.* Titling your work is not unlike naming a pet. You want people to notice it and think you made a good choice.

✏ PROOFREAD.

Before turning in your work, proofread it. Proofreading is different from reviewing a draft. When you review, you think of the content of what you wrote and how it sounds. When you proofread, you watch for grammatical and spelling errors. Check anything that looks odd by using this book or a dictionary. Make sure that every sentence is properly punctuated.

Look for careless errors — mistypings, misspellings,

misnumberings, or format irregularities. These mechanical errors greatly affect how easily your final product can be read. These errors cause a reader to slow down and correct them mentally before being able to continue. They are like road bumps on an otherwise smooth street.

✐ ADD A TOP PAGE.

Your teacher may have a special format for the title page of your paper. If not, you should make sure you have this essential information: title, date, your name, and, if there are several sections of your class, the one in which your paper belongs. If your teacher allows, you may want to use some sort of illustration. Whatever the case, it should say "Come on in."

✐ NEED A FOLDER?

In case you've been preparing your work for a long time, you may feel uncomfortable sending it into the outside world without a jacket. That is why many writers put their work in folders of one sort or another. If someone puts a cup on top of it or it's thrown into a stack or a briefcase, it won't get mussed up. Folders give you one last chance to make your work look as if you care about it. They're not for every assignment — just the special ones.

GIVE YOURSELF A PAT ON THE BACK.

• • • • • • • • • • • • • • • • •

Now that you've turned in your work, perhaps you can remember when it began — with only a topic and a few ideas. Now it's time to congratulate yourself. You're not just a person who puts any old thing on paper, but a careful, style-conscious writer. Producing good writing is probably a lot harder than you imagined, but it has its rewards. Among them may be not just good grades but a sense of pride and a little attention. You may find that people want to read your stories, essays, and poems. They may actually look forward to your reports. Some of the writers whose work was used in this book have won Scholastic Writing Awards. Others are students just like you who have found the pleasures of *Writing With Style*.

BIBLIOGRAPHY

. . . .

Other Sources You Might Use:

Otfinoski, Steven. *The Scholastic Guide to Putting it in Writing.* Scholastic Inc., 1993.

Peck, Richard. *Write a Tale of Terror*. Book Lures, Incorporated, 1987.

Polette, Nancy. *The Best Ever Writing Models*. Book Lures, Incorporated, 1989.

Polette, Nancy. *Write Your Own Fairy Tale.* Book Lures, Incorporated, 1992.

Policoff, Stepan and Skinner, Jeffrey. *Real Toads in Imaginary Gardens: Suggestions and Starting Points for Young Creative Writers.* Chicago Review Press, Inc., 1991.

Tchudi, Stephen and Tchudi, Susan. *The Young Writer's Handbook.* Simon & Schuster/Aladdin, 1987.

Terban, Marvin. *The Scholastic Guide to Checking Your Grammar.* Scholastic Inc., 1993.

Young, Sue. *The Scholastic Rhyming Dictionary.* Scholastic, Inc. 1994.

INDEX

A

Abbreviations,
    consistency 124
    spelling 94–95
About, use and misuse
    of 103
Action, clarity and 30–31
Active voice, use of 31–32
Acts, script writing 68–70
Adjectives, use of 104–108
Adverbs
    subject and verb
      agreement 75–76
    use and misuse of 104–108
Affect,
    use and misuse of 97
Alliteration,
    poetry writing 56
Almost, use and
    misuse of 107
Among, use and misuse of 103
Anyway – anyways,
    use and misuse of 105

Apostrophes 89–91
    contractions 90–91
    plurals 91
    possession 89–90
Appositive (descriptive
    phrase), comma 86–87
As, use and misuse of 104
Assignment,
    planning and 14–15
Audience, genre
    and style 40–41

B

Bad – badly,
    use and misuse of 105–106
Between, use and
    misuse of 103
Bibliography,
    presentation 126–129
Blank verse, defined 15
Book reports, research for 16
    (*See also* Essays)

Book sources,
bibliography 126–127
Brainstorming,
research and 17

C

Can, use and misuse of 98
Cast of characters,
scripts and 67–68
Character development,
fiction writing 61–65
Clarity
essay writing 47
report writing 41–44
writing skills and 30–33
Clauses, comma 87–88
Closing paragraph,
essay writing 52–53
Collective nouns, subject
and verb agreement 75
Comma 82–89
clauses 87–88
descriptive phrase 86–87
introductory phrase 88–89
parenthetical
expressions 87
serial comma 84–86
Compound objects, object
pronouns 80–81
Compound subjects
pronouns 77–78

subject and
verb agreement 75
Computers
editing and 114–116
presentation 122–123
Content, planning and 14–15
Contractions,
apostrophes 90–91
Could of, use and
misuse of 98–99
Couplets, rhyming patterns
poetry writing 57–58
Creative writing,
research for 16

D

Deleting, computer editing 115
Dependent clause,
comma 87–88
Descriptive phrase,
comma 86–87
Devil's advocate position,
essay writing 49–51
Dialogue, script writing 69–70
Dictionary, use of 13, 39
Drafts, editing 112–118

E

Each other, use and
misuse of 109

Editing, 112–118
    computers and 114–116
    described 112–114
    drafts 116–118
Effect, use and misuse of 97
Essays 46–53
    clarity 47
    closing paragraph 52–53
    defined 15
    devil's advocate
        position 49–51
    explanations 48–49
    generalizations 51–52
    opening paragraph 47–48
    purpose of 46–47
    research for 16
Explanations
    essay writing 48–49
    report writing 41–44

F

Farther,
    use and misuse of 106
Fewer,
    use and misuse of 106–107
Fiction, writing of 15, 60–65
    (*See also* Stories)
Final sentence, paragraph
    construction 26
Folders, presentation 131
Footnotes, report writing 44–45

Formatting,
    presentation 123–124
Free verse, defined 15
Further, use and misuse of 106

G

Generalizations,
    essay writing 51–52
Genre, style and 40–41
    different 14–15
Goes, use and misuse of 99
Grammar 71–81
    computer editing 116
    pronoun selection 76–81
        (*See also* Pronouns)
    subject and verb
        agreement 72–76
        (*See also* Subject and
        verb agreement)

H

Handwriting, presentation 120
Hanged, use and
    misuse of 99–100
Headings
    described 34–35
    format 124
    use of 35–37
Healthy – healthful,
    use and misuse of 107

Herself, use and
    misuse of   109–110
Himself, use and
    misuse of   109–110
Hung, use and
    misuse of   99–100

I

Imagery, poetry writing   54–56
Indefinite pronouns,
    subject and
        verb agreement   73–74
Independent clause,
    comma   87–88
In – into,
    use and misuse of   104
Interest, report writing   46
Internet sources,
    bibliography   128–129
Intervening phrase,
    subject and
        verb agreement   73
Interview sources,
    bibliography   129
Introductory dependent
    clause, comma   88
Introductory phrase,
    comma   88–89
Irregular verbs,
    use and misuse of   96–97

Its – it's, use
    and misuse of   110

L

Lay, use and misuse of   100
Less, use and
    misuse of   106–107
Lie, use and
    misuse of   100–101
Like, use and misuse of   104

M

Magazine sources,
    bibliography   128
May, use and misuse of   98
Metaphors,
    poetry writing   54–55
Most, use and misuse of   107

N

Negative forms, clarity and 33
Nouns, collective, subject
    and verb agreement   75
Number,
    singular and plural   72

O

Object pronouns,
    described   80–81

Off – off of, use
    and misuse of   108
One another, use
    and misuse of   109
Onomatopoeia,
    poetry writing   55
Opening paragraph,
    essay writing   47–48
Outlines,
    planning methods   20

P

Page numbers,
    presentation   125
Paragraphs,   22–30
    as building blocks   28–30
    construction of,   24–26
    essay writing
        closing paragraph   52–53
        opening paragraph   47–48
    speaker changes and   28
    structure of   23–24
    (*See also* Sentences)
Paraphrasing
    plagiarizing contrasted   46
    of sources   44
Parenthetical expressions,
    comma   87
Passive voice, use of   32–33
Personification,
    poetry writing   56

Phrase
    descriptive, comma   86–87
    introductory, comma   88–89
Plagiarizing, paraphrasing
    contrasted   46
Planning   9, 11–20
    assignment
        and content   14–15
    methods of   18–20
    overview of   11–12
    research and   16–17
    timing and
        workplace   12–13
Plays
    defined   15
    script writing   66–70
Plurals
    apostrophes   91
    subject and
        verb agreement   72
    (*See also* Subject and
        verb agreement)
Poetry   54–60
    defined   15
    imagery in   54–56
    research for   16
    rhymes   56–58
    verses   59–60
Polishing   71–118
    adjectives and
        adverbs   104–108

Polishing *(continued)*
  editing   112–118
    (See also Editing)
  grammar   72–81
    pronoun selection   76–81
    (See also Pronouns)
    subject and verb
      agreement   72–76
    (See also Subject and
      verb agreement)
  overview of   71–72
  preposition use
    and misuse   102–104
  pronouns   108–112
    (See also Pronouns)
  punctuation   82–94
    apostrophes   89–91
    commas   82–89
    quotation marks   92–94
    (See also Punctuation)
  spelling   94–95
  verb use and misuse 96–102
Positive forms,
  clarity and   33
Possession,
  apostrophes   89–90
Practice, writing skills
  and   21–22
Prepositions
  object pronouns   80–81
  use and misuse   102–104

Presentation   119–132
  bibliography   126–129
  folders   131
  formatting   123–124
  handwriting versus
    machine writing 120–123
  overview of   119–120
  page numbers   125
  proofreading   130–131
  reading aloud   129
  sections   126
  spacing   124–125
  table of contents   126
  title pages   131
  titles   130
Production   21–70
  clarity   30–33
  essay writing   46–53
  fiction   60–65
  genre and style   40–41
  overview of   21–22
  poetry writing   54–60
  punctuation and
    headings   34–39
  report writing   41–46
  scripts   66–70
  sentences and
    paragraphs   22–30
  thesaurus and
    dictionary use   39
Pronouns   76–81

compound subjects   77–78
indefinite, subject and
   verb agreement   73–75
object pronouns   80–81
subject pronouns   77
use and misuse of   108–112
verbs of being   78–79
Proofreading,
   presentation   130–131
Protagonist,
   fiction writing   61
Punctuation   82–94
  apostrophes   89–91
    contractions   90–91
    plurals   91
    possession   89–90
  commas   82–89
    clauses   87–88
    descriptive
      phrase   86–87
    introductory
      phrase   88–89
    parenthetical
      expressions   87
    serial comma   84–86
  described   34–35
  purposes of   82–84
  quotation marks   92–94
    spoken words   92
    written words   93–94
  run–on sentence   38

Q

Questions, subject and
   verb agreement   76
Quotation marks   92–94
  spoken words   92
  written words   93–94

R

Reading aloud, proofing   129
Real – really, use
   and misuse of   108
Reports
  defined   14
  research for   16
  writing of   41–46
Research, planning and   16–17
Resolution,
   fiction writing   61
Reviews, defined   14
Rhymes, poetry writing   56–58
Run–on sentence, dangers
   and correction of   37–38

S

Said, substitutes for   99
Scenes, script writing   68–70
Science project reports
  research for   16
  writing of   42–44

Scripts 66–70
   cast and 67–68
   format of 66–67
   organization of 68–70
Sections, presentation 126
Sentences 22–30
   compound subjects,
     pronouns 77–78
   paragraphs and 26–28
   punctuation of 82–89
     (See also Punctuation)
   structure of 23
     (See also Paragraphs)
Serial comma, use of 84–86
Set, use and
   misuse of 101–102
Settings, script writing 69
Similes, poetry writing 54
Sit, use and misuse of 101–102
Sources
   bibliography 126–129
   footnotes 44–45
   paraphrasing of 44, 46
Spacing, presentation 124–125
Speaker changes,
   paragraphs and 28
Spell checking,
   computer editing 115–116
Spelling
   quotations 94
   standardization 94–95

Spoken words,
   quotation marks 92
   dialogue 66, 69–70
Stories
   defined 15
   research for 16
   (See also Fiction)
Style, genre and 40–41
Subject(s)
   compound
     pronouns 77–78
   subject and verb
     agreement 75
   sentence structure
     and 23
Subject and verb
   agreement 72–76
   collective nouns and 75
   compound subjects and 75
   indefinite pronouns
     and 73–74
   intervening phrase and 73
   questions and 76
   singulars and
     plurals and 72
   there and 75–76
Subject pronouns
   described 77
   verbs of being 78–79
Subtitles,
   use of 35–37, 124, 126

T

Table of contents,
   presentation   126
Tense, clarity and   30–31
Text moving, computer
   editing   116
That, use and
   misuse of   110–111
Themselves, use
   and misuse of   109–110
There, subject and verb
   agreement   75–76
Thesaurus, use of   39
Timing, planning and   12–13
Title pages, presentation 131
Titles, presentation   130
Tools, planning and   13
Topic sentence, paragraph
   construction   24–25
Typewriters,
   presentation   121–122

V

Variety, use of   39
Venn diagrams,
   planning methods   19
Verbs
   of being, pronouns   78–79
   sentence structure and, 23

subject and verb
   agreement   72–76
   (*See also* Subject
      and verb agreement)
   use and misuse of   96–102
Verses, poetry writing   59–60

W

Wait on – wait for,
   use and misuse of   102
Who – whom,
   use and misuse of 110–112
Word clusters,
   planning methods   18–19
Word processor
   editing and   114–116
   presentation and   122–123
Words in series,
   commas   84–86
Workplace, planning and 12–13
Would of, use and
   misuse of   98–99
Writing skills
   planning   11–20
   polishing   71–118
   presentation   119–132
   production   21–70
   stages approach to   9
Written words, quotation
   marks   93–94